The Pictish Conquest

THE BATTLE OF DUNNICHEN 685
& THE BIRTH OF SCOTLAND

About the Author

James E. Fraser is Lecturer in Celtic and Early Scottish History & Culture at the University of Edinburgh. His other books include *From Caledonia to Pictland: Scotland to 795*, and *The Roman Conquest of Scotland: The Battle of Mons Graupius AD 84*, also published by Tempus. He lives in Edinburgh.

Praise for JAMES E. FRASER

17.99

'524 3325 3

'resh interpretation of why the Romans invaded and' *THE SCOTS MAGAZINE*

'nges a long held view... the battle for ownership is Graupius will be almost as hard fought as the clash' *THE SUNDAY EXPRESS*

The Pictish Conquest

THE BATTLE OF DUNNICHEN 685
& THE BIRTH OF SCOTLAND

JAMES E. FRASER

TEMPUS

Dedicated to the dear memory of my friend, Rhianon Shepherd.

Considerate, quam admirabilis sit aer,
et recolite quam inscrutabilia sunt iudicia Dei.

This edition first published 2006

Tempus Publishing Limited
The Mill, Brimscombe Port,
Stroud, Gloucestershire, GL5 2QG
www.tempus-publishing.com

© James E. Fraser, 2002, 2006

The right of James E. Fraser to be identified as the Author
of this work has been asserted in accordance with the
Copyrights, Designs and Patents Act 1988.

British Library Cataloguing in Publication Data.
A catalogue record for this book is available from the British Library.

ISBN 0 7524 3962 6

Typesetting and origination by Tempus Publishing Limited
Printed and bound in Great Britain

Contents

Acknowledgements

This book is the culmination of a decade of interest in the battle that I knew first as *Nechtanesmere*; I owe a debt of gratitude to Alexander Callander Murray, whose Honours classes at the University of Toronto awakened that interest, along with my ongoing fascination with things Pictish. The idea for the project came from Jonathan Reeve at Tempus, who has remained the driving force behind it, and I am grateful to Alex Woolf for suggesting that I take it on and for giving me access to works in advance of publication. In writing the book and understanding its place in Dunnichen historiography I have profited from the work of Graeme Cruickshank, and also from an engaging discussion with him on the subject. Our understandings of the battle and its significance differ in many ways, but such divergence of opinion and interpretation have not lessened my estimation of Mr Cruickshank's important contributions to Dunnichen scholarship over the past twenty years. The attractive reproduction of the Dunnichen symbol stone, used as the cover illustration, was generously provided by Leslie Reid of Strathmiglo; it is but one piece from his extensive collection of such reproductions of early insular art, some of which can now be enjoyed (and purchased) at www.ancientstoneart.com. My first excursion into Forfarshire was made possible by Karen Hartnup; those photographs that are not the fruits of that trip I owe either to three years' worth of excursions with Alex Woolf or to the generosity of Gary and Margaret Dixon with their automobile. Richard Oram has kindly offered his time and expertise in order to strengthen my understanding of the developing topography of Angus and Forfarshire – imperfections in that understanding, however, are my responsibility alone.

My greatest debt is owed to Morgyn Wagner for the encouragement and support she has provided throughout this project, for help with the photography and maps and for commenting upon the book in draft.

JEF
St Drostan's Day
July 2002

List of Abbreviations

ACamb 'Annales Cambriae', John Morris (ed.), *Nennius: British History and the Welsh Annals* (London & Chichester, 1980), 85–91. Cited by year.

AClon 'Annals of Clonmacnoise', Denis Murphy (ed.), *The Annals of Clonmacnoise, being annals of Ireland from the earliest period to A.D. 1408* (Lampeter, 1993). Cited by year.

Adomnán, VC Adomnán, *Vita Columbae*, Alan Orr Anderson and Marjorie Ogilvie Anderson (eds), *Adomnán's Life of Columba* (Oxford, 1991). Cited by book and chapter.

AI: 'Annals of Inisfallen', Seán Mac Airt (ed.), *The Annals of Inisfallen* (Dublin, 1988). Cited by year.

Anderson, *ESSH* 1: Alan Orr Anderson, *Early Sources of Scottish History A.D. 500 to 1286*, vol. 1 (Edinburgh, 1922).

Anderson, *KKES*: Marjorie Anderson, *Kings and Kingship in Early Scotland* (Edinburgh and London, 1973).

Anon., *VCA*   Anonymous, *Vita Sancti Cudberti*, Bertram Colgrave (ed.), *Two Lives of Saint Cuthbert* (Cambridge, 1940). Cited by book and chapter.

ASC   *Anglo-Saxon Chronicle*, Michael Swanton (ed.), *The Anglo-Saxon Chronicles* (London, 2000). Cited by year.

AT   'Annals of Tigernach', Whitley Stokes (ed.), *The Annals of Tigernach*, vol. 1 (Lampeter, 1993). Cited by AU year.

AU   'Annals of Ulster', Seán Mac Airt and Gearóid mac Niocaill (eds), *The Annals of Ulster (to A.D. 1131)* (Dublin, 1983). Cited by editorial year.

Bede, *HE*   Bede, *Historia Ecclesiastica Gentis Anglorum*, Bertram Colgrave and R.A.B. Mynors (eds), *Bede's Ecclesiastical History of the English People* (Oxford, 1991). Cited by book and chapter.

Bede, *VCP*   Bede, prose *Vita Sancti Cuthberti*, Bertram Colgrave (ed.), *Two Lives of Saint Cuthbert* (Cambridge, 1940). Cited by chapter.

FA   'Fragmentary Annals', Joan Newlon Radner (ed.), *Fragmentary Annals of Ireland* (Dublin, 1978). Cited by section.

HB   *Historia Brittonum*, John Morris (ed.), *Nennius: British History and the Welsh Annals* (London and Chichester, 1980). Cited by section.

HDE   *Historia Dunelmensis Ecclesiae*, attributed to Simeon of Durham, T. Arnold (ed.), *Symeonis Monachi Opera Omnia*, vol. 1 (Edinburgh, 1882). Cited by book and chapter. For an English translation of this work, see J. Stevenson (ed.), *Simeon's History of the Church of Durham* (Lampeter, 1993).

HR   *Historia Regum*, attributed to Simeon of Durham, T. Arnold (ed.), *Symeonis Monachi Opera Omnia*, vol. II (Edinburgh, 1882). Cited by year. For an English translation of this work, see J. Stevenson (ed.), *Simeon of Durham: A History of the Kings of England* (Lampeter, 1987).

Stephan, *VW*   Stephan the Priest, *Vita Sancti Wilfrithi*, Bertram Colgrave (ed.), *The Life of Bishop Wilfrid by Eddius Stephanus* (Cambridge, 1927). Cited by chapter.

Tacitus, *Agricola*   Cornelius Tacitus, *De vita Iulii Agricolae*, R.M. Ogilvie and Sir Ian Richmond (eds), *Cornelii Taciti de vita Agricolae* (Oxford, 1967). Cited by chapter.

I

Introduction

Saturday 20 May 685 is one of the earliest firm dates in Scottish history. It entered the historical memory of the insular peoples because, according to a contemporary witness, based probably in the monastery of Iona, 'the battle of *Dún Nechtain* was fought' on that day, 'in which Ecgfrith son of Oswig, the Saxon king (*rex Saxonum*), who had completed the fifteenth year of his reign, was killed with a great body of his soldiers by Bridei son of Beli, king of Fortriu (*rex Fortrenn*)'.[1] The latter kingdom at the time probably encompassed (roughly) what is now the Tayside administrative region of eastern Scotland.[2] Its native population were members of the ethnolinguistic group known to modern scholars as Picts, and although 'Verturian'[3] identity was destined to disappear from the political map of early historic Britain in the tenth century, Fortriu was one of the most prominent of insular kingdoms in the eighth and ninth centuries. Recent scholarship has pointed to the likelihood that the emergence of the Pictish kingdom of Fortriu as a dominant force in northern British affairs began in the reign of Bridei, and this has underlined the need to revisit the events and significance of 20 May 685 afresh. This book represents an attempt to meet such a need by considering not just the battle itself, a subject fraught with difficulties, but also the historical and political context within which the men of Fortriu won their most famous military victory.

Bridei and his Verturian countrymen may be suspected of having referred to the location of this clash of arms in their own language not as *Dún Nechtain*, which is a Gaelic place-name meaning 'fortress of Nechtan', but as *Linn Garan*, a Brittonic place-name preserved in a ninth-century source and thought to mean 'crane lake'.[4] Similarly, the defeated *Saxones*, who in fact were probably almost entirely men from the northern Anglian kingdom of Bernicia (encompassing roughly the present Lothian, Borders, Northumberland, Cumbria, and Durham administrative regions and some part of Dumfries and Galloway), also appear to have remembered the battle of 'crane lake' as having occurred at a body of water which they seem to have called *Nechtanesmere*, the 'mere' or lake of Nechtan.[5] The stronghold of Dún Nechtain has, since the nineteenth century, been identified fairly conclusively with Dunnichen Hill to the east of the burgh of Forfar in Angus, but the battle itself entered into antiquarian discourse under its Anglian name, so that as late as 1985 it was still as the battle of *Nechtanesmere* that the Verturian victory was commemorated in Scotland on its thirteen-hundredth anniversary. Since then, however, scholarly convention has been shifting in accordance with the view of Graeme Cruickshank, the subject's most prolific modern scholar, that the battle ought to be explicitly identified with Dunnichen Hill where it was fought, and which since 1991 has been threatened by the spectre of quarrying.[6] In this study we shall accordingly speak of the events of 20 May 685 as the battle of 'Dunnichen', preferring this to the more traditional 'Nechtanesmere' and the more appropriate (arguably) 'Linn Garan' or 'Dunnichen Hill', while also eschewing, for reasons that will become apparent, the label 'Dunnichen Moss' that has emerged in recent times.

Precious little information of the kind required by the military historian survives from 20 May 685, yet the battle of Dunnichen has been characterised as 'one of the biggest clashes of arms in the history of "Dark Age" Britain',[7] and as a decisive moment in insular history which, among other things, 'paved the way for northern Britain to become the independent nation of Scotland and not merely an extension of England'.[8] Whether or not it is appropriate to attach such significance to this single event, it has been because of such views that the battle has sustained the interest of successive generations of commentators, and it will be necessary here to put such long-standing views to the test. Some of the arguments that follow will place the battle into a political and historical context that may please few of its most ardent enthusiasts, but others may agree that grandiose interpretations of the battle of Dunnichen have contributed too little to our understanding of its immediate causes and effects, and that these are worthy of more close consideration than they have yet received. The relative value of the literary sources from which we have any hope of recovering such information or reconstructing the battle itself has been discussed at great length on more than one occasion, most recently by Professor Leslie Alcock.[9] It has been deemed worthwhile to collect the main literary evidence here for readers to consider in a series of appendices, but there seems little need to rehearse here a subject to which the present author has little to offer, save perhaps that we ought to note that where evidence is available it is always open to interpretation.

Indeed, our most exciting and visually appealing source by far for the battle of Dunnichen is also, unfortunately, the most difficult to come to grips with, and interpretation of its testimony can be undertaken only with caution. It consists of an upright slab of red sandstone standing over seven feet in height in the kirkyard of Aberlemno, some three and a half miles north of Dunnichen Hill, upon one face of which a battle-scene was carved in Pictish times.[10] Of itself this 'cross-slab' in its entirety is truly a Scottish treasure, being 'one of the most remarkable relics' of its kind among a number of similar monuments that have survived in Scotland from the Pictish period.[11] In addition, however, Cruickshank, its most avid student in recent times, has put forward what seems to me a thoroughly compelling case for believing that the monument is more important still as a relic of the Pictish past because its battle-scene is 'a lithic record of the battle of Dunnichen'.[12] Such an interpretation of the Aberlemno battle-scene is, as Cruickshank has freely conceded, ultimately impossible to prove, and there is no getting around the fact that our underlying uncertainties mean that the battle-scene can never provide decisive evidence on its own. Nevertheless, so painstaking has been Cruickshank's examination of the wide range of evidence pertaining to the monument, and so determined have been his efforts to answer sceptical objections, that the battle-scene cannot be ignored as a potential source of additional information about the nature of the battle of Dunnichen and its utility in this regard seems to be acquiring increasing acceptance among scholars.[13]

Its context aside, at least two rather different theories about the general course of the battle have emerged in recent years, neither of which can be demonstrated categorically to provide the definitive model for the actual events of 20 May 685. We shall see that there is good reason, at least to my mind, to prefer one theory over the other, but this is not the same thing as decisive proof: we cannot at present identify the exact location of the fighting with complete confidence, and neither can we hope to provide a blow-by-blow account of the melee save in a work of fiction. These are truisms which at the present time leave no room for argument, and nothing that follows here will change this. However, the evidence is such that an impressionistic reconstruction of the battle is quite possible, while the reasons outlined here, including the importance attached to the engagement as early as the eighth century, would seem to demonstrate that such a reconstruction, however inexact and open to interpretation, is probably worthwhile. It is because of such considerations that this book has been undertaken with the view that it is possible, despite the limitations of our evidence, to offer something concrete on this subject to Dunnichen enthusiasts, to historians of the period, and to a general readership alike.

Ecgfrith and Bridei – *Fratrueles* and Foes

We know that Ecgfrith son of Oswig was forty years old when he was killed in the battle of Dunnichen;[1] this means that he was born between 21 May 644 and 20 May 645. His birthplace was somewhere in the Bernician kingdom, perhaps at its principal stronghold on Bamburgh Rock (*Bebbanburg*). The catalogue of his maternal and paternal forebears reads like a veritable list of the most illustrious historic figures in the first century of English Christendom. His mother Eanfled, who as Oswig's queen was to prove a formidable figure in Northumbrian politics in her own right, was the daughter of the great Deiran King Eadwini (616–633). His kingdom encompassed roughly what are now the administrative regions of Humberside and North, West and South Yorkshire, though he exercised control over the Bernicians and *imperium* or indirect authority over a number of other kingdoms, and his role in bringing the Christian religion into what became northern England was the subject of much of the second chapter of Bede's

Ecclesiastical History of the Anglian Nation.[2] Eanfled was his daughter by his Kentish Queen Æðilburga,[3] whose father Æðilberct was the first of the Anglo-Saxon convert kings of the sixth and seventh centuries, at whose invitation St Augustine established his missionary church at Canterbury in 597.[4] Oswig, Ecgfrith's father, was the son of Aeðilfrith, the pagan Bernician king who drove Eadwini into exile and seized control over Deira in 604, only to be killed in battle with the East Angles twelve years later, paving the way for Eadwini's kingship. In 645 when Ecgfrith was born, Oswig had only recently become king of the Bernicians – the third of Aeðilfrith's sons to succeed him – having succeeded his elder brother Oswald after his death in battle with Penda, king of the Mercians, at *Maserfelth* in August 642.[5]

Penda, like Oswald before him, is referred to as *rex Saxonum* ('king of Saxons') in the generally contemporary record of the Irish annals,[6] and there can be little doubt that, at the time of Ecgfrith's birth, this renowned pagan king exercised *imperium* over both Oswig and the Deiran King Oswini son of Osric.[7] As a boy, perhaps in the aftermath of a certain 'battle of Oswig against Penda' in 650 when he was five years old,[8] Ecgfrith was taken to live as a hostage of the Mercian king. He seems to have been placed in the keeping of Penda's Queen Cynewise until her husband was killed by the Bernicians at the battle of the *Winwed* on 15 November 655.[9] Among other things, this decisive victory enabled Oswig to tighten his grip on the Deiran kingship, over which he had begun to assert a degree of authority after King Oswini was murdered by Oswig's *praefectus* in 651 and the Bernician king was able to secure the succession of his nephew Oidilwald son of Oswald.[10] When Oidilwald failed four years later to support his uncle against Penda at the *Winwed*, the victorious Oswig seems to have engineered his removal from the kingship of the Deirans and to have arranged for Ecgfrith's step-brother Alchfrith to succeed him.[11]

Alchfrith was Oswig's elder son by a previous marriage,[12] and there was no doubt an increasingly keen rivalry between him and Ecgfrith as the younger step-brother grew to manhood in the late 650s. As the eldest of the sons of their father's current and active queen, Ecgfrith was in an ideal position to inherit Oswig's Bernician kingship and the wider hegemony he had built from Bamburgh, and could also exploit his mother's Deiran heritage to undermine Alchfrith's position. It must therefore have been an unsettling development in the eyes of the Deiran king when, according to a chronology recoverable from Bede and the *Anglo-Saxon Chronicle*, Ecgfrith, then about fifteen years old, was married in 660 to Aeðilthryð, the widowed daughter of the East Anglian king, a union destined to end in 672 when Aeðilthryð elected to retreat into monastic life at the Bernician monastery of Coldingham.[13] The threat posed by Ecgfrith to his future is quite likely to have been a key factor in the deterioration of Alchfrith's relationship with his father. The end result was a violent clash in the middle of the 660s from which Oswig emerged victorious and from which Alchfrith does not emerge at all in our literary sources – an act of suppression that was presumably intended to preserve the reputation of Oswig, and which must make us suspect that Alchfrith's fate was an unpleasant one.[14] In the aftermath of these grim developments Ecgfrith probably – but not certainly – acquired the vacant kingship of his mother's people through the intervention of his father, serving as Oswig's sub-king for about four years before succeeding to his own Bernician heritage when Oswig passed away in February 670, the first and only seventh-century king of the Bernicians or Deirans to die of natural causes.[15]

From about the age of twenty, then, Ecgfrith may be thought to have begun building up his military experience with an eye towards his eventual succession to the kingship of the Bernicians. The extent to which he did so in these early years of his career can, however, only be guessed at. Having been freed from his Mercian captivity in 655, he may have earned his spurs on seasonal campaigns mounted in the interests of pushing the frontiers of his father's *imperium* westward into the Solway area. It seems reasonable to suppose that he was also present at Oswig's side when the king went to war with Alchfrith, much as the latter had himself stood with his father at the *Winwed* a decade earlier.[16] As king of the Deirans Ecgfrith may have led his own campaigns into the British territories of what are now the administrative regions of Cumbria and Lancashire north of the Ribble. Certainly by the early years of his Bernician kingship there seem to have been significant Anglian conquests in these territories, some of which lands he donated to the church of Ripon, along with 'consecrated places in various parts which the British clergy had deserted when fleeing from the hostile sword wielded by the warriors of our own nation'.[17]

Ecgfrith may, then, have been a veteran warrior and experienced military commander when he fought in his first attested battle. The date of this engagement is uncertain: we know only that it took place soon after he had become king of the Bernicians in 670, and that it appears to have preceded the end of his marriage to Aeðilthryð in 672.[18] His adversaries were 'bestial Pictish populations (*populi*)' whose leaders may be thought to have looked upon the death of the hegemon Oswig as an opportunity 'to throw off from themselves the yoke of servitude' which had been in place since the Bernicians, at some unknown date, had 'subjected to Anglian rule the greater part of the Pictish people'.[19] Later events indicate, as we shall see, that it was some or all of the territory now encompassed by the Central and Fife administrative regions of Scotland that were subdued and annexed by Oswig – lands that had previously probably been held in subjection by the kings of Fortriu, the existence of whose kingdom is first attested in this period.[20] It would seem, then, to have been Ecgfrith's continuing *imperium* over this region that was being challenged in this first of his known battles, almost certainly under the leadership of the Verturian king Drust son of Donuel.[21] In answer, the Bernician king 'immediately prepared a mounted force (*equitatus exercitus*), being a stranger to tardy efforts', and rode north, where he encountered 'an enormous and, moreover, a hidden enemy', for the Pictish leaders had 'gathered together innumerable nations (*gentes*) from every nook and corner in the north'.[22]

This description of Ecgfrith's Pictish enemies in Stephan's *Life of Saint Wilfrith* is very important. It reminds us that (in this period at least) the application of such Latin terms as *Picti*, *Angli*, *Britanni* and *Scotti* in insular writing to denote particular ethnolinguistic groups cannot be taken as indicating anything like political unity among the Picts, Angles, Britons or Gaels. In the time of Ecgfrith and Bridei, each of these groups appears instead to have consisted of several – even 'innumerable' – kingdoms, *gentes* ('nations') and *populi* ('peoples'), some of which Pictish ones appear to have joined forces to make war upon Ecgfrith in the early years of his reign.[23] Though significantly outnumbered as a result, Ecgfrith and his men attacked 'and slew an immense number of people, filling two rivers with the corpses of the slain, so that (marvellous to relate) the slayers, passing over the rivers dry-foot, pursued and slew a crowd of fugitives'.[24] We do not know which rivers are the ones in question, but it seems very likely that this engagement at the Two Rivers provides us with some of the details surrounding what we know otherwise to have been 'the expulsion of Drust from the kingship' in 671.[25] In other words, it may be thought to have been as a result of this decisive Bernician victory that Drust son of Donuel was removed from power in Fortriu.

Drust's successor, according to the same regnal list, was Bridei son of Beli, king of Fortriu and victor of Dunnichen. The Gaelic poem *Iniu feras Bruide cath*, attributed to Riagail of Bangor, says the following in reference to this victory:

Iniu feras Bruide cath	Today Bridei gives battle
im forba a senathar,	over the land of his grandfather,
manad algas lá mac Dé	unless it is the wish of the son of God
conid é ad genathar.[26]	that restitution be made.

Another Gaelic poem, this one preserved in the tenth-century *Life of Adamnán*, notes that Bridei's father Beli had not been king of Fortriu like his son, but a king of Dumbarton (*rígh Ala Cluaithi*),[27] the conspicuous rock at the mouth of the River Clyde upon which in the seventh century stood the principal stronghold of an important British kingdom, the extent of which is not certain. The implications of these poetic references are that Bridei's claim to the Verturian kingship that he acquired in 671 descended not from Beli, his father, but rather from his paternal grandfather, who, according to a Welsh genealogical tract clearly associated with the kingdom of Dumbarton, was called Neithon map Guithno.[28] The 'Pictish' regnal list confirms that there was indeed a Pictish (probably Verturian) king called *Nectu* who appears to have reigned from 599 to 619, and who may therefore be identified with Neithon map Guithno, although the list gives him the designation 'descendant of Uerb' (*nepos Uerb*). This is not the place to rehearse the evidence relating to the kingship of Neithon map Guithno and his *nepotes Uerb* kindred: it will suffice to point out that it is quite reasonable to suspect, although it is not certain, that his son Beli was the 'Belin' whose obituary appears in the 'Annals of Wales' under the year 627.[29] This would require Bridei map Beli to have been born no later than 628 and to have been at least fifty-seven years old at Dunnichen when he gave battle 'over the land of his grandfather', all of which chronology is perfectly viable.

For our present purposes, the most interesting and intriguing fragment of information available to us about the familial background of Bridei map Beli is that, according to material included in the ninth-century *History of the Britons*, he and Ecgfrith were *fratrueles*,[30] specific Latin kinship terminology that denotes cousins who were the sons of two brothers, but which by the early medieval period could also be used to denote cousins who were the sons of two sisters.[31] The more traditional interpretation of this term as it pertained to Ecgfrith and Bridei has been dogged by the persistence of the matrilineal model of Pictish succession – the idea that Pictish men traced their heritage through their mothers rather than through their fathers. This model will not allow these two men to have been actual *fratrueles*, requiring that the term be applied instead as loosely as the word 'cousin' is sometimes used by modern English speakers. It has usually been thought in consequence that the term refers to common kinship with Oswig's elder step-brother Eanfrith son of Aeðilfrith, who became king of the Bernicians in 633, apostatised and was killed in 634, and whose son Talorcan reigned as a king in Pictavia in the 650s.[32] Ecgfrith was undeniably Eanfrith's nephew, and various genealogies have been constructed in which Bridei appears as the apostate's great-grandson or, more believably, as his grandson.[33]

The matrilineal model has, however, been justly and convincingly criticised in a succession of recent studies.[34] In the most comprehensive of these, Alex Woolf has shown that, once matriliny is left aside as an academic red herring, it is perfectly possible to apply *fratruelis* literally as indicating that Beli of Dumbarton 'was married to a daughter of Edwin [Eadwini] of Deira, an option which presents no difficulties, chronological or otherwise'.[35] There are indeed other good indications that Bridei and Ecgfrith were thought to have been very closely connected, and that this connection was widely appreciated among insular commentators. One Irish annal reference to the 'great battle' of Dunnichen gives the misleading but interesting impression that it was an internal squabble 'between the Picts', while the *History of the Britons* is further suggestive of the same kind of thing, characterising this engagement between *fratrueles* as *gueith* or 'strife' rather than as a *bellum* or battle.[36]

Such kinship is emphatically no guarantee of friendship or partisanship, but the combination of Bridei's relationship with Ecgfrith and the circumstances through which the former seems to have acquired the Verturian kingship in 671 provides much to commend Woolf's suggestion that this king of Fortriu was 'helped into his kingship by Ecgfrith' in the wake of the Bernician king's great victory at the Two Rivers.[37] In return for such assistance, which no doubt included the provision of armed support, Ecgfrith would presumably have expected that his *fratruelis* would provide unswerving loyalty as his sub-king. The situation envisioned here puts one in mind of the events of 616, when the army of Rædwald, the powerful king of the East Angles, defeated and killed Oswig's father Aeðilfrith in battle at the River Idle, thus enabling Eanfled's father Eadwini, who was then in the protection of Rædwald, to acquire Aeðilfrith's kingships of the Bernicians and Deirans.[38]

Having succeeded in affirming and perhaps even extending his *imperium* over his father's Pictish dominions, Ecgfrith was soon forced to meet a challenge of a different sort, this time from south of the Humber. In 673 or 674,[39] the Mercian king Wulfhere son of Penda, who in the late 650s had succeeded in ending Oswig's *imperium* over his kingdom, 'roused all the southern peoples' against the Bernicians and the Deirans and their new king and over-king, 'intent not merely on fighting but on compelling them to pay tribute in a servile spirit'.[40] Ecgfrith proved able to deal with this threat of subjugation to Wulfhere in decisive fashion once again, putting Wulfhere's army to flight, killing 'countless numbers' of his men, and turning the tables by placing the Mercians under tribute (*sub tributo*), which gives us some indication of the nature of the obligations that the Bernician king had imposed upon the Verturian Picts a few years earlier. The succession of Ecgfrith to the kingship of the Bernicians and the over-kingship of the Deirans, then, involved a baptism of fire in which his mettle, his military acumen and, perhaps most importantly, the faithfulness of his followers, were put to the test. Such remarkable success on the battlefield against his two most prominent neighbours, and against forces that, even if we must suspect a degree of exaggeration on the part of Stephan, are nevertheless likely to have outnumbered his own, would seem to speak well of Ecgfrith on such counts. There are indications in our evidence that some of his military success in this critical period may be credited to the efforts of talented subordinates – perhaps men who could call upon combat experience acquired while fighting alongside Oswig in his campaigns of the fifties and sixties. At the Two Rivers, for example, 'the brave sub-king Beornheth' is singled out by Stephan for the support he provided in securing the Anglian victory, while the same source credits a measure of Ecgfrith's success in the war against Wulfhere to 'the advice of elders' (*consilium senum*).[41] The Bernician king was evidently a capable and formidable adversary who knew the value of seeking advice and support, and who his foes underestimated at their peril, and this is an important point to which we shall return in our attempts to reconstruct the general course of the battle of Dunnichen.

Clearly Ecgfrith had become a seasoned warrior and captain when, in 679, probably in late August or early September,[42] he fought a 'serious' (*gravis*) battle against Wulfhere's brother and successor as king of the Mercians, Aeðilred son of Penda. This engagement took place on the banks of the River Trent where fortune was less kind to Ecgfrith, for his younger brother Aelfwini, then about eighteen years old and seemingly his brother's Deiran sub-king, was killed in what appears (despite the coyness of our northern literary sources) to have been a significant defeat.[43] In the aftermath of this battle, according to Bede, Archbishop Theodore intervened from Canterbury to broker a peace settlement between the two powerful kings which seems to have required Ecgfrith not just to relinquish his *imperium* over the Mercians themselves, but also to restore to their own *imperium* the territories he had acquired from Wulfhere earlier in the decade, in return for which he received due compensation for Aelfwini's death.[44] We must balance such evidence alongside Stephan's rather euphemistic comment that Ecgfrith was 'a stranger to tardy efforts', a characteristic which Bede, in his more charitable moments, described as 'daring' (*ausus*), and, when he was inclined to be more critical, as 'rashness' (*temerarius*).[45] Despite such characterisations, and more recent assertions that he 'was compelled not only to maintain but to extend his father's conquests' and spent his time 'in continual warfare, hopping from one beleaguered frontier to another',[46] Ecgfrith seems to have been quite capable of taking advice and exhibiting forbearance and restraint when necessary, as in the case of the peace settlement after the battle of the Trent. It is probably worth adding, moreover, that each of these key battles fought by Ecgfrith in the 670s appears to have been intended to protect lands and rights that he already possessed, rather than acts of aggression intended to extend his *imperium* into new territories that had not already been added to the hegemony he inherited from his more aggressive father.

Aeðilred's victory cut off the northward flow of southern tribute which had been enhancing Ecgfrith's resources for some five years. It also proved, of course, that the Bernician king – who with the death of Aelfwini appears to have assumed (or resumed) direct rule over the Deirans, thus bringing into being what Bede called the kingdom of the Northumbrians (*regnum Nordanhymbrorum*) which endured into the eighth century[47] – was not invincible. Stephan makes it clear, however, that in Fortriu Bridei was content to remain at peace with him, such that his kingdom 'remained in subjection, under the yoke of captivity, until the time when the king was slain'.[48] Yet there are important indications that, though he seems to have remained steadfast in his tributary and other obligations as sub-king, the Verturian king did indeed take notice of Ecgfrith's troubles. Indeed, it may be thought that the seeds of the strife that was to bring the two *fratrueles* into conflict at Dunnichen were sown six years earlier at the Trent, about which Stephan wrote a generation later that St Wilfrith had prophesied to his opponents that 'you shall then weep bitterly over your own confusion'.[49] No doubt Bridei, who as we have seen may have been twenty years or more older than his *fratruelis*, had acquired some degree of military experience of his own in the years before acquiring the Verturian kingship in 671. There is even a possibility that he had been living in exile among the Bernicians or Deirans for some time before the battle of the Two Rivers, and he may have campaigned with Oswig or Ecgfrith against their enemies. At any rate, in marked contrast to the first seven years of his reign, the years after 679 seem to have been characterised by notable instability north of the Forth, punctuated by attacks on the stronghold of Dunnottar in Kincardineshire in 680 or 681, on the Orcadian islands, which 'were annihilated by Bridei' in 681 or 682 (*deletae sunt a Bruide*), and on Dundurn, a stronghold at the foot of Loch Earn in upper Strathearn in 682 or 683.[50]

It was on the heels of these episodes that the battle of Dunnichen was fought in 685, and it is possible that it was not entirely unrelated to them. Bridei himself is explicitly mentioned as a party to the conflict in only one of these prior campaigns, but we may suspect that he was in fact involved in all of them. Indeed, it has been suggested by Woolf that this succession of Pictish clashes represents the undertaking of an aggressive programme by which Bridei sought successfully to extend his own *imperium* beyond the bounds of Fortriu into more northerly and westerly regions of Pictavia, installing 'tributary structures and mechanisms of over-lordship learned from the kings of Bamburgh' in order to take the first steps towards 'the creation of a Verturian hegemony amongst the Picts' on the Bernician model.[51] It may be thought, in other words, that, whatever his past combat experience, in the years immediately prior to Dunnichen, Bridei was busily engaged in establishing his influence and authority beyond his frontiers, organising Verturian military campaigns into regions as far afield as Orkney and Strathearn and adding to his personal prestige through a string of battlefield successes that also gave him access, by way of tribute, to greater resources. It is both interesting and highly suggestive that this aggressive period in Bridei's reign seems to have begun in the wake of Ecgfrith's defeat on the Trent, and it is difficult not to suspect that the Verturian king seized upon the opportunity to take advantage of the difficulties and distractions of his Anglian over-king, even if all indications are that Fortriu continued dutifully to convey the necessary tribute southwards throughout this period.

Such a model is attractive on a number of levels, not least because it offers a ready explanation as to why Stephan and Bede give the impression that, in the time of Ecgfrith, his Pictish opponents belonged to 'countless *gentes*' and 'kingdoms' (*regna*),[52] yet could be referred to a generation or two later as a single *gens* living either in the *regiones* of the single southern Pictish kingdom (*prouincia*) identifiable as Fortriu or else in one of the Pictish kingdoms (*prouinciae*) north of the Mounth.[53] In another study it has been argued by the present writer that Canterbury's decision in 681 to transfer Anglian ecclesiastical jurisdiction over this Pictish *prouincia* from the see of Hexham/Lindisfarne to a new see at Abercorn in West Lothian may also be interpreted in the light of Bridei's aggressive activities, having perhaps been arranged as a result of close co-operation between the archbishop and the Northumbrian and Verturian kings.[54] This development has formerly been interpreted as a step towards more intensive Anglian control over Bridei's kingdom, enabling Ecgfrith to 'monitor the Britons and Picts' and to 'ensure the channelling of Northumbrian influence among the Pictish clergy and their aristocracy'.[55] It seems to me, however, that such a view fails to take sufficient account of the fact that implicit within these events is a recognition on the part of Canterbury – and seemingly also on Ecgfrith's part – of a distinct single Pictish ecclesiastical zone worthy of its own bishop. Even if the creation of this new Pictish see was not done largely at Bridei's request, it may certainly be seen as having played into the hands of the king who has been identified as having been responsible for the development of 'a new more centralised kingdom' of Fortriu, the emergence of which changed the political landscape of Pictavia and required the aforementioned terminological changes describing its population.[56]

Although there can be little doubt that their kingdom was tributary to Ecgfrith, in the final analysis any assumption that, in the period between the battles of the Two Rivers and Dunnichen, the Verturian Picts were a people preoccupied with their oppressed state and fixated upon avenging a catalogue of indignities suffered at Anglian hands does them little justice. There would seem, in other words, to have been nothing particularly inevitable about the battle of Dunnichen. If it serves to intensify the magnitude and drama of the Verturian achievement on 20 May 685, to envision the battle as the logical climax of a story that began with the first Bernician incursions into British territory, casting the Verturian army as the rock against which this wave of 'remorseless Northumbrian advance'[57] was finally broken, the resulting impression of Bridei's victory and its significance can only be misleading. A strong argument can instead be made that Bridei and his *fratruelis* were on excellent terms from the outset of the former's kingship, and it may be thought that they maintained a close and fruitful relationship from which both profited until Ecgfrith was defeated by the Mercians at the Trent in 679. One might suggest that goodwill between them may have lasted as late as 681 and the appointment of Trumwini to the see of Abercorn, though by this time Bridei appears to have departed from his prior routines and to have been pursuing an aggressive and expansive policy that Ecgfrith cannot have failed to notice, however preoccupied he may have been with his own affairs.

All indications are that Fortriu continued to pay dutiful tribute to the Northumbrian king, but Ecgfrith and his counsellors must nevertheless have noted the extent to which Bridei's star had risen in comparison with Ecgfrith's own since Aeðilred's victory. No doubt the prescient among them began to suspect that a time might soon come when Bridei would seek to change his relationship with Ecgfrith – or perhaps even to be released from his obligations outright. In neither eventuality would war be necessary in principle. An exchange of daughters between Penda and Oswig in the days of Ecgfrith's boyhood saw Alchfrith marry Penda's daughter Cyniburg and Peada son of Penda marry Oswig's daughter Alchfled,[58] which has been interpreted as an initiative to diffuse the growing tensions between an over-king (Penda) and his increasingly ambitious sub-king (Oswig).[59] In the event, this earlier strategy appears to have brought about only a temporary respite in the ongoing strife between Penda and Oswig, but we must not lose sight of the fact that going to war in seventh-century Britain was an act of will, and that honourable alternatives to fighting did exist if the parties to a dispute were inclined to pursue them. That Ecgfrith and Bridei chose not to pursue such alternatives is clear, and if their war was inevitable, that inevitability was rooted in the immediate needs of one or both protagonists, and not in the nature of their societies or the course of sixth-century political history.

3

On the Warpath

The reasons for Ecgfrith's fateful excursion into Fortriu to make war upon Bridei in the spring of 685 are not clear, and will never be certain. Our Northumbrian narrative sources are unanimous in their agreement (in hindsight) with the anonymous hagiographer of Lindisfarne, who wrote in his *Life of Saint Cuthbert* that his king had been killed at Dunnichen 'in accordance with the predestined judgement of God'.[1] Such a view, once it had gained currency among Northumbria's clerical intellectuals, can hardly have spoken well for Ecgfrith's real motives. It is therefore not at all surprising that these earliest commentators demonstrate very little interest in remembering or considering what these motives were. Instead, we find the 685 campaign described as 'the time when King Ecgfrith was marauding and laying waste to the Pictish region',[2] or when he 'had taken an army against the Picts and was devastating their kingdoms with cruel and savage ferocity'.[3] The point of such moralistic language in describing Ecgfrith's behaviour was to emphasise that, whatever may have been his actual intentions and whatever else he may have been engaged in, as he advanced into Fortriu he was inviting the doom that was visited upon him by God. As far as our authorities were concerned, the proof of the merits or demerits of such questionable activities on the part of kings was in the proverbial pudding: had Ecgfrith won the battle of Dunnichen there would have been few Northumbrian clerics who doubted that God had deigned that the Verturian Picts should suffer his 'cruel and savage ferocity' as just punishment for their sins. As it happened, however, Ecgfrith was defeated and killed, and his destruction demonstrated conclusively according to the analytical mentality of the contemporary clergy that the campaign of 685 had been 'an unjust invasion'.[4]

Clearly we must therefore be wary of following our sources too closely in their appraisal of Ecgfrith's motives and the propriety of his behaviour. As a seventh-century insular king, Ecgfrith had a solemn obligation 'to protect his people against the depredations of their neighbours and to lead them on expeditions of plunder and conquest'.[5] It is likely that his motives in making war upon the men of Fortriu were more complex than this or than emerges from our texts, but at least we need not follow the latter blindly in their suggestion that there was anything particularly untoward or immoral about either Ecgfrith's aggressive behaviour or his activities while on campaign. It is true that Bede illustrates Ecgfrith's folly by alleging that his friends and counsellors, among whom was St Cuthbert whose tomb is now in Durham Cathedral, were troubled by his decision to make war upon Bridei and implored him not to undertake this campaign.[6] It is impossible to know the extent to which such a claim may have been similarly influenced by hindsight of the 'I-told-you-so' variety (much less by a desire to affirm the prescience of Cuthbert and the unacceptability to God of Ecgfrith's designs). If it has any kind of historical accuracy, Bede's evidence here would seem to underline the suggestion put forward above that in 685 war was probably not Ecgfrith's only option in dealing with Bridei. This point seems to run through our literary evidence in its insistence that the decision to make war upon the Picts was rash on this occasion. It is a claim which, unlike the more dubious accusation of injustice, allows for the likelihood that Ecgfrith was faced with a real and significant problem with regard to Bridei 'which called for his urgent intervention',[7] but did not necessarily require the armed response for which he opted.

With admirable caution, Peter Marren has suggested that in Fortriu 'there had, presumably, been some form of rebellion against Northumbria on a scale which required the king's personal intervention'.[8] This, provided we allow for considerable leeway in how we interpret 'rebellion' while acknowledging the suggestion of our sources that 'the king's personal intervention' need not have involved an invasion, would seem quite sound as a starting point. By reading between the lines of our literary authorities we may think it highly unlikely that such a 'rebellion' involved a massing of Verturian forces on the Northumbrian frontier, much less a Verturian invasion or even more informal Pictish raiding of Northumbrian soil,[9] since threats of this kind can hardly have invited anything other than the armed response upon which our sources frown so vociferously.

On the other hand, it has been argued in the preceding chapter that the underlying cause of the *gueith* or strife that arose between the two *fratrueles* and former friends in 685 is likely to have been significant shifts which appear to have occurred in their relative levels of their prestige after Ecgfrith's defeat in the battle of the Trent in 679 and Bridei's subsequent successful campaigning early in the 680s. Such a state of affairs was bound to make a Verturian king intent upon extending his *imperium* among the Picts think twice about the amount of tribute he continued to send southwards. It is also likely to have raised Ecgfrith's suspicions that the conspicuously active Bridei might seek such a change in their relationship by curtailing his tribute payments or by withholding them altogether. In such a scenario, the required nature of Ecgfrith's response to a 'rebellion' of this kind in Fortriu would have been decidedly more murky and open to interpretation than can have been the case if the Verturian king had simply taken up arms against his over-king. The idea that his *fratruelis* had failed – or else had expressed his unwillingness – to go on honouring his tributary or other obligations to Ecgfrith would seem more in the spirit of our sources than the idea of an armed Verturian 'rebellion'. It seems to me that this makes the former preferable as a hypothesis in any consideration of the motives that underpinned Ecgfrith's invasion of Fortriu in 685.

All of this must call into question any assumption that, throughout the first fourteen years of his reign, Bridei single-mindedly devoted all of his efforts towards freeing himself from Ecgfrith's over-lordship. In such a scenario, the Verturian king may be seen as spoiling for a war with his *fratruelis* that would prove 'the culmination of his campaigning – the objective which all his efforts had been dedicated to achieve'.[10] We have seen how problematic it has become, however, to accept without qualification the age-old and emotive idea that, in the period of the Oswegian hegemony, 'the southern Picts had become an oppressed people' who, after the Two Rivers, 'were reduced to a state of slavery'.[11] Instead, although there can be little doubt that he remained subject to Ecgfrith until 685, Bridei map Beli, far from being a paragon of resistance to Anglian oppression, may be thought to have been something of its instrument. There is every likelihood that as Verturian king he took a great deal of advantage of a position that he probably owed to his *fratruelis* in the first place, and for which he was apparently happy enough to pay, at least initially, in the form of tribute. It is therefore interesting to consider the possibility that Bridei's aggressive behaviour in the early 680s was undertaken – outwardly at least – in the very name of extending Ecgfrith's Pictish *imperium*. This, like so much pertaining to the Picts, cannot be demonstrated to any conclusive degree, but at least it may be said that it is probably a misleading assumption that would characterise what appear to have been the first steps towards Verturian hegemony as 'a bid to regain his nation's freedom' organised with a mind towards ensuring Fortriu's 'readiness for the great test against the Northumbrians'.[12] Such a view would seem calculated to advance the figure of Bridei of Fortriu as an anachronistic defender of the freedom and independence of Scotland, and takes too little account of the evidence that suggests on the contrary that the Verturian king acted with a degree of caution in mounting his 'rebellion', and that it was not he but his *fratruelis* who was spoiling for a fight in 685.

It would seem to offer little to our understanding, then, to wax dramatic about an innocuous Pictish people chafing under the yoke of a high-handed Anglian oppressor with a deep-seated, even biological imperative to suppress all things Celtic. Neither is it particularly helpful to suggest that at issue in the 680s 'was whether the eastern half of north Britain would be ruled by the English or the Picts'.[13] This may arguably be one approach to conceptualising the general course of Northumbrian and Verturian history between the seventh and ninth centuries as a whole, but with specific reference to Dunnichen it misrepresents the nature of Dark Age kingship and *imperium*. Bede does make it fairly clear that until his death at Dunnichen Ecgfrith exerted direct authority over some undefined Pictish territory (*terra*) 'which was being held by the Angles'.[14] The likelihood, however, is that this *terra* lay between Fortriu and Bernicia along the Forth frontier and by the time of Oswig had not yet been annexed into the kingdom of Fortriu, though the Picts who lived in this frontier zone may formerly have been subject to Verturian *imperium* in some way.[15] Indeed, Bridei's very presence in Fortriu is proof that Ecgfrith, though he was Bridei's over-king, did not rule the kingdom directly, and – unless we are to believe that it was his intention in 685 to eliminate Bridei and to assume the Verturian kingship himself – had the Northumbrians won the battle of Dunnichen their king is highly unlikely to have ruled Fortriu thereafter.

No doubt a victorious Ecgfrith would have acted much as he had when Drust was expelled from his kingship in

671, exerting his influence to have Bridei removed from power and replaced by some viable successor who could be counted on to rule in Fortriu as a more dutiful sub-king. At issue in 685, then, was not whether Fortriu or Northumbria was going to emerge as the dominant power in northern Britain, but the future of Bridei map Beli – whether he was destined to become an independent king and over-king in his own right or a victim of his own ambitions. Above all else the events surrounding the battle of Dunnichen represent a personal struggle in which two powerful potentates vied with one another over the future of their relationship. Neither is likely to have spared a great deal of thought towards the ramifications of their actions for future generations in northern Britain, or even, perhaps, towards the future well-being of his respective kingdom, nation or people.

If, as suggested above, the outcome of the battle of the Trent in 679 provided the clash between Ecgfrith and Bridei with its genesis, it is possible that particular events in 684 brought matters to a head. Stephan reports that after his disastrous encounter with Aeðilred on the Trent, Ecgfrith 'gained no victory until the day of his death'.[16] The Irish annals, however, record that in June 684 – less than a year before Ecgfrith's death – 'Saxons lay waste to the plain of Brega and many churches', and Bede relates of this same year that Ecgfrith 'sent an army to Ireland under his *dux* Berct', which 'wretchedly devastated a harmless nation that had always been most friendly' and 'spared neither churches nor monasteries'.[17] The reasoning that lay behind this expedition into the modern Irish county of Meath is even more obscure than Ecgfrith's motives for invading Fortriu in the following year, and the episode has long been one of the great enigmas of Ecgfrith's reign. Professor Thomas Charles-Edwards has drawn attention to the real possibility that Ecgfrith had inherited from Oswig something like papal sanction – perhaps even papal encouragement – to make war upon and 'bring into the orthodox fold' any insular kingdom which persisted in refusing to adopt the universalist method of calculating the date of Easter that Oswig himself had accepted in 664.[18] Brega was the home territory of Fínsnechtae Fledach, who at the time ruled as over-king over the southern branch of the powerful Uí Néill, an extended kindred which held authority over much of the northern half of Ireland and had not, probably, been persuaded as yet to abandon the traditional method of calculating Easter. Thus Professor Charles-Edwards's arguments would seem, if they are accepted, to provide insight into the way in which Ecgfrith may have justified Berct's expedition in general, and the damage inflicted upon the churches and monasteries of Brega in particular, yet the matter of his direct motives for attacking when and how he did remain open to question.

Only one of the handful of versions of the Irish annals (based ultimately upon a common source containing contemporary information) contains any reference to a potential motive, testifying that Berct attacked Brega because of 'the alliance of the Irish with the Britons'.[19] The identification of the Britons in question is anyone's guess,[20] but if this annal is to be believed we must presume that, whoever they were and wherever they lived, Ecgfrith had recently been making war upon them, inspiring them to look across the Irish Sea to Fínsnechtae Fledach for support. Berct's expedition into Meath, then, was no mere raid in pursuit of hostages and easily-won booty, but a calculated political act on the part of his king. It has been variously suggested that Ecgfrith's intention was to extend his *imperium* across the Irish Sea,[21] but had this been the case one might have expected that he would have conducted the campaign himself rather than entrusting it to a deputy. At any rate, it would seem the most straightforward reading of the annal evidence to suppose that the attack on Brega was a punitive strike intended to intimidate Fínsnechtae Fledach and to dissuade him from supporting his British allies, and to suppose that it was as surety against any Uí Néill initiative to become further involved in his British wars that Ecgfrith welcomed the taking of hostages in 684.[22] We need not, in other words, seek to explain Berct's expedition by imagining that Fínsnechtae Fledach and the Uí Néill had become involved in some elaborate plot either to challenge Ecgfrith's *imperium* over Dál Riata, the Gaelic kingdom encompassing roughly the Argyll and Bute Region, or to topple Ecgfrith himself from power by supporting a rival claim to his kingship.[23] This latter hypothesis has acquired a certain amount of recent currency, but to the present writer it probably makes too much of what appears to have been a highly questionable claim on the part of Ecgfrith's successor Aldfrith to have been eligible to succeed him.[24] It would seem important to remember that in June 684 no one will have had any particular inkling that the Northumbrian king, who was not yet forty, would be dead without an heir in less than twelve months' time.

Whatever the reason for the Irish expedition, and however justifiable it may have been with recourse to the Easter question, it is clear from Bede that Ecgfrith received a considerable amount of criticism from churchmen as a result of this episode. Indeed, it is possible to read the testimony of the Gaelic poem *Iniu feras Bruide cath* as suggesting that such a backlash motivated the king to make some kind of public show of remorse, for the poet says of his death at Dunnichen that 'even though he did penance, it was penance too late'.[25] Whatever form such a response to his critics might have taken it appears to have been in vain, the proof of which being, once again, in the proverbial pudding. Both Bede and *Iniu feras Bruide cath* indicate that in the aftermath of Ecgfrith's death it was believed – with the benefit of hindsight, of course – that it had been because Berct's Irish victims sought divine vengeance 'with unceasing imprecations' that Ecgfrith was killed at Dunnichen in the year after the expedition to Brega. As Bede saw it, 'one may believe that those who were justly cursed for their wickedness quickly suffered the penalty of their guilt at the avenging hand of God',[26] and this is mirrored in the belief of the Gaelic poet that 'Christ has heard our prayer that Bridei would avenge Brega'.[27] There need not have been any real connection between these two events to justify the one made by contemporary clerics, yet it remains a possibility that Bridei made some use of the perceived injustices of Berct's expedition to justify his 'rebellion' – probably involving a cessation of the flow of Verturian tribute into Northumbria and perhaps nothing more than that.

The possibility that events in Meath in central Ireland can have influenced the king of Fortriu in eastern Scotland is not as far-fetched as it might first appear – nor does it require us to envision an alliance between the Uí Néill and Bridei. There is every chance that some Verturian churches felt a measure of fellowship with Irish churches that had suffered from Northumbrian afflictions in 684. We know too little about contemporary churches in Fortriu to be certain about this, but it may be pointed out that St Vigeans, near the modern burgh of Arbroath on the Angus coast, is universally suspected 'to have been a religious centre of outstanding importance' in Pictish times,[28] and bears a Pictish dedication to St Féichín, the patron and former abbot of the monastery of Fore (*Fobar*) in Westmeath.[29] How early this dedication may be is not certain, but the existence of such ecclesiastical connections between Fortriu and Meath allow for the very real possibility of outrage on the part of some Verturian church leaders at the events of Berct's expedition in 684. If the Verturian king was already contemplating 'rebellion' by then, an official expression of protest against the Brega expedition would no doubt have proved handy both in any attempt to justify his disloyalty and in presenting an ideal moment to 'rebel'. The possibility that Bridei chose to construe his activities in 685 as a manifestation of his kingdom's disappointment with regard to the attack on Meath would provide us with one explanation of the connection that our sources make between Berct's activities and the battle of Dunnichen. It remains entirely possible, however, that this connection was more imagined than real.

However we envision the immediate background to the battle of Dunnichen, we can only theorise about Ecgfrith's reasons for choosing to resolve the Verturian problem through military means when others appear to have thought it unnecessary. It probably does us little good to characterise Ecgfrith and the other seventh-century Bernician kings as 'hungry for conquest',[30] for in so doing we would have to recognise that their Pictish, Gaelic and British counterparts were surely no less 'hungry', even if their respective appetites were of necessity curbed by the fear of biting off more than could be chewed. That the Bernicians were more successful in extending their lordship than their neighbours is no guarantee that those neighbours were not just as committed to do the same. The career of Bridei as sub-king would seem to be proof enough of that, and we have no creditable grounds for believing that Ecgfrith was significantly more belligerent than any other contemporary king. Indeed, we have seen that our literary evidence creates the general impression that Ecgfrith was more concerned with protecting the frontiers he had inherited from Oswig than with expanding them: on the other hand, there can be little doubt of the aggressive policy adopted by Bridei in the early 680s.

It has been suggested that making war upon Bridei was an act of pure aggression on Ecgfrith's part, whether in the interests of filling coffers that had become too depleted by the demands of retainers and the Church or as 'an attempt to consolidate Northumbrian power over the Picts'.[31] The present writer is more inclined to believe, however, that, as appears to have been the case in his clashes with Drust, Wulfhere and Aeðilred, Ecgfrith was probably provoked to action by developments in Fortriu that he construed as a threat to his rights as over-king. This having been said, concerns surrounding his ability to command the necessary resources to satisfy his retinue and his Church may well have been a factor in Ecgfrith's decision to choose the military option over whatever alternatives were proposed by his counsellors. Since 679 he had been recovering from the battle of the Trent while his people adjusted – a quarter-century after the death of Penda – to the spectre of a resurgent and aggressive Mercia. Neither he nor his father had ever held *imperium* over the Mercians for a length of time that would have been long enough to allow them to become so dependent upon Mercian tribute that its cessation (in Ecgfrith's case after the battle of the Trent in 679) would have greatly undermined their lordship. However, it would be understandable if Ecgfrith felt particularly vulnerable to Aeðilred in the period after his defeat, and so particularly sensitive to any development – like some proposed reduction or complete cessation of tribute from Fortriu – that might tip the balance of power in favour of the Mercians.

In other words, it is possible that Ecgfrith and some, at least, of his advisors simply did not feel as though Northumbria was in a position in the 680s to be as reasonable in its dealings with a restless Bridei as Penda had been in the 650s when he attempted to reach a rapprochement with Oswig. On a related point, Ecgfrith may also have expected that a decisive victory over the Picts, and especially upon a Pictish kingdom on the rise, might serve to buoy the spirits of men who had been humiliated on the Trent and to restore something of their former confidence in him as their king. After all, his victory at the Two Rivers in 671 must have had important positive effects upon the confidence of the Northumbrians who fought alongside their new king in battle with Wulfhere a year or two later, and Ecgfrith may have hoped that history would repeat itself once he had returned triumphant from the north in 685. It is unlikely that Ecgfrith was alone and unilateral in such thinking. The grim fate of churches in Meath in the previous year, however, provides a ready explanation as to why some key Northumbrian church leaders might have spoken ill of an invasion of Fortriu. There can be little doubt, as discussed above, that our sources would have suppressed some or all reference to such criticism had things turned out differently for Ecgfrith, and chose to focus upon it for reasons of hindsight. This is not to say, however, that we ought not to believe the very idea that Cuthbert and others begrudged the king his decision to make war. Indeed, the recent example of Meath must have loomed large in the thinking of a man like Cuthbert, who in his younger days had formed a relationship with Pictish clerics and had even visited their churches – churches for the safety of which the new bishop of Hexham must have justifiably feared.

From the point of view of the military historian, it is unfortunate that our early commentators were more concerned with emphasising the moral justice of Ecgfrith's destruction than with outlining the political and other factors which convinced him that it was imperative that he go to war in 685. As a result his real motives all but elude us. In this chapter an attempt has been made to arrive at a handful of impressionistic conclusions on this subject through a close reading of the literary evidence. No doubt both Ecgfrith and Bridei had complex and multi-faceted reasons for behaving as they did in the period leading up to the Northumbrian invasion of Fortriu. It does neither of them justice to portray them one-dimensionally, the one as a remorseless oppressor and the other as a dauntless champion of liberty. In the final analysis it seems most likely that war was not Ecgfrith's only option in seeking to resolve this crisis, and that he chose to fight for a range of specific reasons that were reasonably rational – although it remains a possibility that his kinship with the Verturian king exacerbated any feelings of betrayal he might have experienced. Some of his familiars were evidently dissatisfied by his decision, and though this dissatisfaction was expressed by later writers on purely moral grounds, those who opposed the invasion probably had their own range of reasons. Ecgfrith would not, however, be stayed, and may be thought to have undertaken his campaign as something of an act of distraint, intended on the one hand to exact tribute personally that had not been sent southwards by Bridei, and on the other to punish the Verturian king for having failed to honour his obligations to his over-king. These are the issues that are most likely to have brought the two *fratrueles* to Dunnichen in May 685, and it may be doubted if either spared much thought for anything so grandiose as the future governance of the diverse peoples of northern Britain.

4

The Road to Dún Nechtain

In the last few months prior to his death, Ecgfrith appears to have been quite busy dealing with Northumbrian ecclesiastical matters. At some point between the beginning of 685 and the inception of his doomed Verturian campaign he presided over a church synod at *Tuifyrdi* on the River Aln in Northumberland, whence he was required to take ship to the Farne Islands off the Bamburgh coast to compel Cuthbert, the future saint living in hermitage on the Farne, to accept the synod's appointment to the see of Hexham.[1] The king was accompanied in this voyage by Trumwini, the Bishop of Abercorn on the Firth of Forth, who was almost certainly one of the seven bishops who subsequently joined Ecgfrith in bearing witness to Cuthbert's episcopal consecration at York during the Easter festival on Sunday 26 March.[2] These events of March would have provided the future saint with an ideal opportunity to join his voice to those others that advised the king against an invasion of Fortriu. We ought probably to presume, then, that the planning for this campaign across the Forth had begun before Easter. It may even have begun at, or as a result of, the synod of *Tuifyrdi*, allowing Ecgfrith to consult with Trumwini of Abercorn, whose recent interactions with Bridei and the *prouincia Pictorum* must have provided the organisers of the campaign with invaluable information. Indeed, if the Verturian tribute was normally sent to Ecgfrith by way of Abercorn it is possible that it was Trumwini who was the bearer of the bad news to his king regarding the Verturian 'rebellion'. A month later on Sunday 23 April – four weeks less a day before his death – Ecgfrith was at Jarrow on the Tyne, where he attended the dedication of the church of this new monastery (where Bede was to live and work) to St Paul.[3] It cannot have been much later than this date that the king began his northward journey towards the Forth frontier, probably with Trumwini in tow. If by attending the dedication of the church of Jarrow he was acting in direct anticipation of the invasion that was just about to commence, Ecgfrith was hardly the last English king to begin a Scottish campaign with a very public act of piety.

Unlike the Roman general Agricola, governor of the Roman province of Britannia near the end of the first century, whose excursion across the Forth was prefaced by fleet movements 'to reconnoitre the harbours' of the native population, Ecgfrith is unlikely to have made significant (if any) use of sea power in launching his Verturian invasion in 685. Instead, the likelihood, as we shall see, is that he assembled an *equitatus exercitus* – a 'mounted force' – as he had done in preparation for the Two Rivers campaign in 671 and again for his campaign against the Mercians not long afterwards.[4] A hundred years earlier, a host on a roughly comparable mission of aggression was led southwards out of Dál Riata by the Gaelic King Áedán mac Gabráin to campaign in Manau in the Forth valley. This earlier army is described by Adomnán, the Abbot of Iona at the time of the battle of Dunnichen, as having won a Pyrrhic victory in a battle in which just over 300 of Áedán's men were slain.[5] If this example may be used to provide a rough estimate of the size of such expeditionary forces, it is reasonable to suggest that in May 685 Ecgfrith did not lead much more than about twice this number of Northumbrian horsemen northward to the frontier region along the Firth of Forth. Indeed, such evidence as survives from the period suggests that even at full strength the average Northumbrian *exercitus* of the day will have consisted of 'hundreds rather than thousands of warriors' called to arms by their king.[6]

Those who were obliged to answer such a royal summons to war in seventh-century Northumbria included on the one hand the king's household warriors – his *tutores* and *ministri*. These appear for the most part to have been young, unmarried men 'who, having as yet no land of their own, resided with their lord' the king.[7] In addition, men who had once been household warriors of this kind but had since married and retired to live on an estate given to them by the king remained obliged to answer their lord's summons to arms.[8] Ecgfrith could not, in other words, depend upon the support of a 'national levy' of all Northumbrian freemen to fight for him in his wars – only those men over whom he exerted direct lordly influence were beholden to him in this way.[9] The surviving evidence suggests, as we have seen and will see, that in actual fact the king assembled a body of perhaps 500 or 600 specialised fighting horsemen, rather than mustering every man who was obliged to come when he called. Indeed, if the king acted with the same degree of haste that is implied by Stephan in his account of the battle of the Two Rivers, it might be wondered whether his *equitatus exercitus* of 685 consisted of much more than his young household warriors – the 'members of the royal house' who we know died at Dunnichen with Ecgfrith.[10] The virtues of such haste for a strategist in Ecgfrith's position were that it afforded the enemy, who because he was defending his kingdom is likely to have been able to rally much greater numbers of men to support him, as little time as possible to rally the fullness of his own landed retinue and additional levy. This was probably a consideration of much strategic importance when contemplating an invasion of this kind in this period.[11] Although he must have expected that he would be outnumbered in any event in any battle in Fortriu, Ecgfrith probably took a great deal of solace in the fact that those who did accompany him northwards were experienced fighting men over whom he exercised direct lordship and so expected the highest degree of personal loyalty.

It is possible that as Ecgfrith advanced between Bamburgh and the Forth he supplemented this expeditionary force to some extent through recourse to his landed retainers whose estates lay along the way. Among the latter may have been at least one sub-king: 'the brave sub-king Beornheth' is said to have supported Ecgfrith in his victory over the Picts at the Two Rivers fourteen years earlier, and it has been suggested that he and his son Berctred, who was killed fighting the Picts in 698 (and may also have been the 'Berct' who led the expedition in 684 to Meath), may have been entrusted with the defence of the frontiers of the kingdom and such a position may have required involvement in the Verturian campaign.[12] At any rate, it is generally accepted that like many invaders from the south to come, Ecgfrith's route into Pictavia will have brought his army into the Forth valley to the lowest crossing-point of the river below the Castle Rock at Stirling.[13] In fact, although we cannot press this point to any real length, we may imagine that the Northumbrian campaign of 685 followed much the same route as the much more successful Edwardian Scottish campaign of 1296. In such a scenario, Ecgfrith would have passed through such locations along the way as the monastery of Coldingham (*Coludaesburg*) where his aunt Aebbe was (or had been) abbess and into which his first wife Aeðilthryð had retreated after the battle of the Two Rivers, the stronghold of Dunbar (*Dynbaer*) in East Lothian where a few years earlier he had held St Wilfrith in captivity for nine months when the exiled bishop had attempted to return to his office,[14] and the stronghold of *Eten* upon the Castle Rock at Edinburgh in Midlothian, formerly a British fortress before being captured by the Bernicians in 638.[15]

It seems likely that from Edinburgh the king will have ridden westwards to the monastery and episcopal seat of Abercorn (*Aebbercurnig*) in West Lothian. He may have parted company with Bishop Trumwini here, but there is no particular reason why the bishop cannot have accompanied him on the campaign – it is just possible to interpret Bede's testimony as suggesting that Trumwini was present at Dunnichen. From Abercorn the Northumbrians will have moved on to the stronghold of *Iudeu*, another fortress of British origin that had been in Bernician hands since at least 655 and which stood either on the way to – or more probably upon – the rock of Stirling.[16] The fact that his father had been king of Dumbarton in the first half of the seventh century has raised suspicions among some scholars that Bridei will have exploited this connection in order to make some kind of alliance with his nephew Dumngual map Eugein, then king of Dumbarton and perhaps a particularly formidable figure in northern politics in his own right, or indeed to forge 'a confederacy of British and Pictish tribes'.[17] The possibility that Dumngual loomed as a threat in the west as Ecgfrith rode west from Abercorn must be conceded. Perhaps halfway between Abercorn and Stirling the Northumbrians crossed the River Carron below Falkirk, and it is notable that Dumngual's father and the men of Dumbarton had inflicted a decisive defeat upon the Dál Riata of Argyll in Strathcarron in 642. On the other hand, their kinship does not require us to believe that Bridei and his nephew were natural allies.

The battle of Dunnichen is one of the best documented events in this entire period, and there is no hint of an alliance or of British involvement in Bridei's victory in any of our sources. Only three years earlier, moreover, the men of Dumbarton appear to have been deeply embroiled in the political affairs of northern Ireland, winning a major victory over the Cruithin of Co. Down, and it may have been Dumngual who inflicted a decisive defeat upon the men of Cenél Loairn in Dál Riata a few years previously.[18] All of this suggests that the attentions of the king of Dumbarton were focused upon the greater Firth of Clyde area in the 680s, and it may be thought that he was too preoccupied with Gaelic affairs to present much of a threat to Ecgfrith in 685, however sympathetic he may have been to Bridei's causes.

From the crossing of the Forth at Stirling the likeliest route taken by the Northumbrian expeditionary force will have brought it along the line of the old Roman road over the Ochil Hills and down Strathearn to the crossings of the Rivers Earn and Tay below the Verturian stronghold of Moncrieffe (*Monid Chroib*) on the hill of that name. *Iniu feras Bruide cath* alleges that at Dunnichen Bridei was fighting 'over the land of his grandfather', a reference, as we have seen, to the fact that his grandfather Neithon map Guithno had once been king of Fortriu. There is reason to suspect that this earlier king, who appears to have died around 620, is the man identified by the foundation legend of Abernethy on the Tay as having been that monastery's founder.[19] This allows us to consider the possibility that, as Ecgfrith proceeded down the Earn towards Moncrieffe and the crossing of the Tay at the modern burgh of Perth, he was travelling through (and asserting his *imperium* over) lands that were part of Bridei's patrimony. It may also have been in the environs of Moncrieffe that the Northumbrian king had secured his great victory at 'two rivers' in 671. At any rate Strathearn was probably of immediate relevance to the expedition, and it is likely to have been here in particular, as Marren has suggested, that Ecgfrith set about 'devastating' Pictish territory 'with cruel and savage ferocity' and conducted much of the 'marauding and laying waste to the Pictish region' for which his campaign was remembered in later years.[20] Certainly there is no reason to doubt that this fertile region of Fortriu was 'worth the ravaging',[21] and it has been argued above that, as far as Ecgfrith was concerned, such activity was probably perfectly justified as a form of distraint through which he intended to take for himself – perhaps from Bridei's own lands – what ought to have been forthcoming to him as Verturian tribute.

Thus far there is every likelihood that Ecgfrith and his army were advancing through territory in which the Northumbrians had campaigned *en route* to the Two Rivers in 671, and lands with which some part at least of his men may be thought to have had a passing familiarity.[22] Moncrieffe was a royal stronghold – perhaps the main seat of the Verturian kingship – and even if Ecgfrith himself had never visited Bridei there in all the years of his *imperium*, no doubt Northumbrian visitors to the fortress on various business were not uncommon. Commentators have been almost unanimous in suspecting that having completed his crossing of the Tay at Perth, Ecgfrith will have eschewed the possibility of conducting his men eastwards onto the Carse of Gowrie. The topography of lowland Perthshire and Angus has been much altered by modern improvements that have reclaimed a great deal of land from lochs, swamps and bogs with which Ecgfrith had to contend, and the Carse will simply not have been a viable option. Like Edward I the Northumbrians almost certainly preferred instead to proceed more-or-less along the route followed by the modern A94 between Perth and the burgh of Forfar, in all likelihood following the courses of the Tay and the

Isla as far as Meigle (*Migdele*) in the heart of Strathmore.[23] Today this route follows the course of the Dean Water between Meigle, the site of a major Verturian monastery, and Forfar, but in Pictish times water levels were higher and this route will have been much more treacherous. It followed what was in fact 'a chain of lochs':[24] just down-river from Meigle is Kinloch, a place-name that indicates that it once stood at the head of a loch, now drained, into which the Isla and Dean Water both emptied, while the current Loch of Forfar was considerably more substantial in Ecgfrith's day, extending much further down what is now the upper Dean Water.[25] There is much work to be done on route-ways across the early historic landscape of Fortriu, and the route that a seventh-century invading army will have followed up this difficult section of Strathmore is not entirely clear; it is quite possible that here again it was necessary to follow in the footsteps of the Roman legions in order to skirt these lochs and other hazards. Once we begin to take into account the nature of the topography with which Ecgfrith and his men were faced as they advanced it becomes easier to appreciate how the heart of Angus can have been described to Bede as *inaccessus* ('unapproachable'), while opening up the possibility that it was the bogginess of the terrain, rather than its ruggedness, which gave the Northumbrians the impression of having been 'in a tight place of unapproachable mountains' (*in angustias inaccessorum montium*).[26]

By the time they had reached Meigle, if not before, the invaders were likely to have begun encountering hostile groups of Bridei's men who, Bede relates, 'feigned flight' in order to draw Ecgfrith on to his doom.[27] The details of how this gambit was played out elude us. It is one of the few pieces of information about the campaign that Bede chose to mention, and there has been a certain tendency among scholars to interpret it as a description of the tactical situation at the moment that battle was joined rather than as a reference to a central factor of the campaign in general.[28] Such an interpretation is hardly intrinsically invalid, but it is nevertheless the case that Bede's passing remarks about feigned flight put one in mind of the description of first-century Roman operations in this same country provided by Tacitus. This much earlier account describes how native warriors made a surprise strike against the Ninth Legion before melting away, such that 'marshes and woods covered the enemy's retreat' and prevented the general Agricola from inflicting a decisive defeat upon them.[29] It therefore seems quite reasonable to interpret Bede's evidence as referring to the employment of similar tactics against the Northumbrian expeditionary force in 685, suggesting that, as Sir Frank Stenton wrote, 'like later invaders of Scotland, he [Ecgfrith] was enticed into dangerous country by an enemy which continually gave ground to him'.[30] Though no doubt frustrated by this native strategy, Agricola appears to have remained undaunted and unfooled by it; we need hardly assume that the experienced Ecgfrith was significantly less canny six centuries later. He and his counsellors had, after all, risen to the challenge of matching their wits against Verturian tacticians before, as Stephan points out in his vivid description of the battle of the Two Rivers in 671. On that occasion, Ecgfrith and his 'little band' had been confronted by 'an enormous and, moreover, a hidden enemy', suggesting that Bridei's general strategy fourteen years later may not have been significantly different than that favoured by his predecessor, and that both men employed a general tactical approach to dealing with invasion that had once been used by Agricola's native adversary Calgacus all those years before.

In the final analysis, then, Bede's all too brief description of the Verturian defensive strategy – emphasising the deviousness and slighting the bravery of the enemy – seems by no means conclusive evidence that the battle of Dunnichen took the shape of an 'ambush'. Neither is it any more indicative that Ecgfrith and his captains fell for 'an obvious ruse' than is Tacitus's description of the strategy employed by Calgacus to draw his Roman enemy onto ground of his own choosing for the decisive engagement an indictment of Agricola's battle savvy.[31] Whereas in 84 Calgacus had selected *Mons Graupius* as the place of reckoning in his struggle against the Romans, in 671 Drust had deployed his forces at the Two Rivers mentioned by Stephan,[32] while Bridei map Beli chose to make his stand against his over-king in 'a tight spot' below Dunnichen Hill with its nearby 'crane lake'. Surviving physical evidence for the *dún* or fortress which lent its name both to the battle and to the hill itself is so meagre that its existence has not gone unchallenged. Indeed, were it not for the place-name and the careful detective work of generations of historians faced with difficult literary evidence relating to the battle, we would have very little indication at that a Verturian stronghold once stood upon the hill, much less that it may have been one of the 'seats of Pictish royal power' in Angus.[33] Much more impressive now are the surviving remains of a large stronghold which stood on the summit of the slightly higher Turin Hill just to the north and is now known as Kemp's Castle, thought to have been 'a site of considerable importance' in the Pictish period.[34] It is therefore possible to speculate that it may have been with Kemp's Castle and the royal lands thereabouts in mind as a destination that Ecgfrith rode up the length of the Loch of Forfar until he learned that Bridei had deployed an army a little to the south at Dún Nechtain.

The reliable identification of this battle with Dunnichen Hill goes back no further than George Chalmers in 1807, who supported his hypothesis quite sensibly with reference to early forms of the place-name from charter evidence.[35] It is hardly certain that this was the only Dún Nechtain in Pictavia in 685, but Dunnichen Hill in the heart of Fortriu, surrounded as it is by a preponderance of Pictish antiqui-ties, seems the only credible identification. This having been said, an argument could be made that Kemp's Castle on Turin Hill, if it can be shown to have been occupied in the seventh century, has far greater potential to have been the main royal hilltop settlement in the area, in which case we might imagine that the *dún* on the hill just to the south stood in close association with this more significant site. The traditional identification of *Nechtanesmere* or *Linn Garan* with Dunnichen Moss to the south-east of Dunnichen Hill is, however, much more open to question. Before it was drained in large part about 1760,[36] this moss lay to the east of Dunnichen village below the eastern shoulder of the hill. If Ecgfrith and the Northumbrians were approaching Dunnichen Hill from the direction of the Loch of Forfar to the west, as is generally agreed, it is difficult not to share Professor Alcock's reservations about believing that Dunnichen Moss, which like the modern village of Dunnichen lay on the further side of the hill, is particularly likely to have had anything to do with the battle.

The hypothesis that Dunnichen Moss may be identified as *Nechtanesmere* or *Linn Garan* is generally supported by a series of key assumptions about the battle of Dunnichen, and it is the number of these assumptions, as well as their unsatisfying nature, that undermine the viability of the traditional identification of the 'crane lake'. The first of these is that Ecgfrith and his men were engaged in chasing Picts in 'feigned flight' at the moment that battle was joined. We have already examined and expressed our doubts about the basis of this view, without which there is little reason to suspect that as they advanced up the difficult terrain of Strathmore Ecgfrith and his captains were any less circumspect or cautious than ought to be expected of military leaders of such experience and proven ability. Unless this assumption is made, however, it becomes extremely difficult to explain how 500 or 600 experienced Northumbrian warriors allowed themselves to become bottled up and ambushed between the hill and Dunnichen Moss as is suggested in those reconstructions of the battle that rely upon the identification of the latter as 'crane lake'.[37] Though hardly impossible, such a scenario must be thought extremely unlikely unless we read a great deal into a particular interpretation of Bede's reference to 'feigned flight'. It might be added as a coda that prevailing reconstructions of the battle based upon this ambush model hardly merit the application of the Latin term *bellum* to the engagement when terms like *interfectio* and *strages* were available for use to indicate a massacre.[38]

Still less satisfying are the set of assumptions by which one must explain how a Northumbrian host approaching Dunnichen Hill from the west was manoeuvred to circle the southern slopes of the hill in order to arrive upon its further side, all the while remaining utterly oblivious of the presence of Bridei's army.[39] In addition to making too much again of Bede's 'feigned flight', such assumptions both require a high degree of incompetence on Ecgfrith's part and take too little account of the context within which the battle of Dunnichen was fought. We have no reason whatsoever to suppose that, a generation after Oswig first brought Pictish territory into subjection and more than a decade after the battle of the Two Rivers, there was no one in Ecgfrith's entire entourage who had ever passed that way before and who could therefore have advised the king of the existence of Dún Nechtain on Dunnichen Hill. Even if we do suppose, for argument's sake, that this was entirely alien territory for everyone in the Northumbrian expeditionary force, it is important to be mindful of a story related by Bede about the battle of the Trent in 679 in which it is noted that local peasants appear to have gravitated to the battlefield in order 'to bring food to the soldiers'.[40] It would seem highly presumptuous to assume that Ecgfrith cannot have learned much of what he needed to know, including the existence of Dún Nechtain and the position of Bridei's forces, either by simply monitoring the movements of the local population or indeed through direct interrogation of native informants. There must also have been many visible signs of the deployment of the Verturian army – such things as campfires and the usual array of smells and sounds will have conspired to betray the Pictish position. Finally, it seems reasonable to express doubt as to whether Bridei is likely to have placed the necessary reliance upon – and entrusted his very life to – such an involved and complex strategy as is envisioned by the traditional model. The tactics proposed would have been very difficult to co-ordinate, and the venture carried with it a high element of risk if all did not go according to plan and Ecgfrith managed to avoid falling into such an elaborate trap.

Fortunately, other options lie open to us in our quest to identify *Linn Garan* that allow for Bridei to have employed a more conservative strategy and require neither gross incompetence on the part of seasoned and reasonably capable Northumbrian commanders in hostile territory nor that the Verturian heartland remained utterly alien ground to the Northumbrians after so many years of Bernician *imperium* north of the Forth. It must be stressed, however, that the more traditional identification, however implausible, is not an impossibility, and that our evidence is too poor to disprove any of the assumptions that we have not taken on board here. Perhaps Ecgfrith *was* incompetent – if he were he would not have been the first or last experienced commander to blunder his way to spectacular defeat. Perhaps the Verturian king *did* throw caution and his better judgement to the wind in the interests of risking everything on a deeply complex strategy. It seems to the present writer, however, that any reconstruction based upon such assumptions, though not impossible, takes too much for granted. If, on the other hand, we assume that Ecgfrith and his captains were passably circumspect and accomplished tacticians and that Bridei's plan to bring them to battle was straightforward and relatively conservative, involving minimum levels of complexity and risk, we are still making key assumptions. They may seem on the whole a safer set of assumptions from which to proceed given what we know or can reasonably deduce about the two men and armies involved, but they remain assumptions.

If the circumstantial case against the traditional identification of *Linn Garan* with Dunnichen Moss would seem to be a fairly strong one,[41] it is difficult to accept the argument that the location of the modern village of Dunnichen and its Moss on the east side of the hill can be taken as any kind of indicator that the battle of Dún Nechtain cannot have been fought elsewhere in the general vicinity. The names of both features must be thought to have been derived from the name of Dunnichen Hill itself in comparatively recent times, and while it may be thought most likely that the Anglian place-name *Nechtanesmere* made reference to the same body of water that the Picts called *Linn Garan*, this 'crane lake' too can have been anywhere in the general vicinity of Dún Nechtain, even on the opposite side of its hill.[42] Professor Alcock, undeterred by assertions that the battlefield had been 'located beyond reasonable doubt' when F.T. Wainwright completed his accomplished reconstruction of the extent of Dunnichen Moss in 1948, has indeed drawn attention instead to Restenneth Loch to the north-west of Dunnichen Hill as potentially having been the 'crane lake'.[43] This feature, until it too was drained for its peat and marl in 1788–89 by the same man who began the draining of Dunnichen Moss,[44] was part of the system of lochs and burns lying between Dunnichen Hill and Turin Hill which today form the scattered headwaters of the Lunan Water.

What Professor Alcock has failed to appreciate, however, is that in Pictish times these scattered waters formed a single loch from which Restenneth Loch and what are now Loch Fithie and Rescobie Loch were later formed by a reduction in early historic water levels.[45] This substantial early loch at the head of the Lunan Water, which for convenience's sake we shall refer to henceforth as Restenneth Loch (its identification as *Linn Garan* being but putative), will have lain to the left of any Anglian host advancing towards Dunnichen Hill from the direction of modern Forfar, which lies upon the high ground separating its waters from those of the Loch of Forfar. If Ecgfrith's route up Strathmore lay to the west of the Dean Water, he can only have reached Dunnichen Hill by crossing over this dry ground between Restenneth Loch on his left and the Loch of Forfar on his right, and it is interesting that local tradition believed that a Pictish king was responsible for the construction of a rampart and ditch, long since obliterated, which 'evidently extended from the Loch of Forfar to that of Restenneth'.[46] The following reconstruction of the general course of the battle of Dunnichen (such as it is) will proceed in agreement with Professor Alcock that Restenneth Loch at the head of the Lunan Water, the title to which belonged to the estate of Dunnichen as late as the nineteenth century (though it lay in the neighbouring parish of Forfar),[47] was known to the Picts as *Linn Garan*. It will also proceed in general agreement with Professor Alcock that the battle fought on 20 May 685 in the environs of Dunnichen Hill took place to the north-west of the hill rather than to the south-east of it. It was traditionally held of Loch Fithie, one of the surviving remnants of Restenneth Loch, that in Pictish times a battle was fought 'in this neighbourhood, and probably in the adjoining muir', in support of which it was recorded in the 1790s that 'several large stones, such as are usually found in Scotland commemorative of similar events, are still standing, though without any inscription, not far from the supposed field of battle'.[48] Though intriguing and not to be ignored, such tradition is proof of nothing, and it must be freely admitted in closing that this identification, however reliant upon the rationale put forward above, remains ultimately open to question. Students of the battle of Dunnichen will no doubt continue to align themselves into different camps on this issue, yet the day that new evidence comes to light to provide conclusive proof of the location of the battle will almost certainly be celebrated by all who have an interest in it, regardless of whether one is proven right or wrong.

5

The Battle of Dunnichen, 20 May 685: An Impressionistic Reconstruction

Having examined what may be reasonably recovered regarding the political background of the battle of Dunnichen, and having followed its protagonists onto the battlefield, it can only be with tentative steps that one proceeds to consider what may be reconstructed about the battle itself. Disconnected details of the fighting do survive, but much that we should like to know about it is quite elusive, such that any attempt to understand what happened during the engagement must be a more subjective enterprise than sits comfortably with most historians. Indeed, it might even be thought to be imprudent to engage with this material at all. Yet engage with it we shall, not only in the interests of comprehensive treatment of the subject, but also with a mind towards setting out some kind of alternative model to complement the alternative setting of the battle proposed by Professor Alcock.[1] Readers who, despite the foregoing arguments, will persist in preferring the traditional location and reconstruction of the battle are unlikely to find much that satisfies in what follows here.[2] It is expected, however, that such readers will nevertheless be able to consider the following reconstruction with profit, if only because of its attempt to make use of the impressionistic testimony of the Aberlemno battle-scene to flesh out details that are otherwise all too fleeting.

Foremost among our problems, as we have seen, is the location of the battle. There seems no reason not to accept Chalmers's identification of Dún Nechtain with Dunnichen Hill. The fact that contemporaries associated the battle with this stronghold allows us to suppose that the hill upon which it stood was a significant factor in the battle, probably serving indeed as something of its focal point. Historians of this engagement are, in other words, far better served by their evidence with regard to actually locating the battle than, for example, those of the battle of *Mons Graupius*, the location of which is disputed.[3] On the other hand, we are less well served than historians of the battle of Maldon, which can hardly have taken place anywhere other than the site identified in 1925.[4] We have seen that the traditional identification of the battle-site has placed it on the site of the village of Dunnichen or somewhere in its immediate vicinity, with Dunnichen Moss below it, long since drained, having been identified as *Linn Garan* or *Nechtanesmere*. A preference for Professor Alcock's more logical alternative to this identification has been outlined at some length in the preceding chapter; like him the present writer finds greater interest in the defile formed by Dunnichen Hill and Turin Hill – or to be precise by what are now Green Hill to the south and Pitscandly Hill to the north.[5] The defile itself cannot, however, have been the site of the battle of Dunnichen because of the extent of the waters of Restenneth Loch – the fighting must have taken place to the south of Loch Fithie (a remnant of the former Restenneth Loch), while the association of Dún Nechtain with the battle suggests that the main action took place on the lower slopes of Green Hill. In other words, the present writer would locate the battle roughly on ground over which the A932 now runs between Forfar and the village of Boal, with Loch Fithie to the north and Green Hill to the east. It was here, I suspect, within clear sight of both Dún Nechtain and the major stronghold of Kemp's Castle on Turin Hill, that Bridei deployed his men as rumour of Ecgfrith's approach up the Loch of Forfar reached his ears.

Professor Alcock has rightly reminded us that we have little specific indication in our surviving evidence that the stronghold of Dún Nechtain was itself attacked or besieged as part of the combat.[6] If Bridei planned to make a stand at Dunnichen Hill, it stands to reason that he will have made some attempt to strengthen its hill-top defences, along, perhaps, with those of Kemp's Castle, against the possibility of attack or siege. It is therefore unfortunate that any evidence relating to this with regard to Dún Nechtain has probably long since been quarried away.[7] Nevertheless it is notable that Stephan makes an interesting comparison of the Picts who were defeated by Ecgfrith in 671 with 'a swarm of ants in the summer, sweeping from their hills, [that] heaps up a mound to protect their tottering house'.[8] Such a metaphor may be taken as perhaps hinting at the erection or strengthening of earthworks on the part of the Picts on that occasion. If we reject the possibility of a siege, we may conclude that, as Ecgfrith approached Dún Nechtain from the direction of modern Forfar at the head of both the Loch of Forfar and Restenneth Loch, following roughly the line of the A932 and keeping Restenneth Loch to his left, he found the men of Fortriu deployed on the lower slopes of Green Hill with the *dún* some distance above and behind them, assuming an attitude comparable to that assumed by the native forces of Calgacus at *Mons Graupius*.

The middle row or 'register' of the Aberlemno battle-scene depicts three Pictish footmen standing one behind the other as they prepare to engage the enemy, suggesting perhaps that Bridei arranged his men three ranks deep on the hillside.[9] There is indeed the slightest suggestion here of a slope beneath the feet of these three men, the figure at the rear appearing to stand on slightly higher ground than that in the middle, and the figure at the front appearing to stand on lower ground still. The forward rank depicted on the monument consisted of men armed with a sword of about thigh length and a targe of a size to protect the torso with some kind of spike on the boss. These warriors would seem to have been supported by a rank of men behind them armed with two-handed spears of such length that it could be brought to bear against an opponent who had engaged the forward rank. The men of both ranks appear to be wearing a knee-length hauberk of some description, although these may represent padded tunics rather than mail. Like the rank of men in front of them, the men of the second rank appear to have had targes of similar type. Such spiked shields would no doubt have been particularly useful against mounted opponents, since a horse will have been vulnerable to injury if it found itself driven against the targes of such infantrymen in the press of combat. Similarly, the employment of such long and heavy spears by the men of the second rank indicates that the Pictish infantry depicted in the Aberlemno battle-scene were equipped in anticipation of combat with enemies on horseback whose main form of attack was expected to involve the mounted charge.

The Aberlemno battle-scene, then, allows us to develop an impression of the Verturian force that was fielded by Bridei against the Northumbrians at Dunnichen, as well as providing us with a glimpse of the general nature of the main fighting that took place that day. One is reminded of the opening scenes of *The Battle of Maldon* and the poet's description of how Byrhtnoth, the ealdorman of Essex, 'set about drawing up the men' in readiness to fight an approaching Danish force:

> He rode and instructed, he told the soldiers
> How they should form up and hold the position,
> And he asked that they should hold their shields properly,
> Firmly with their fists, and not be at all afraid.[10]

We have no explicit surviving information to indicate the relative sizes of the forces that were brought to bear against one another at Dunnichen. Stephan informs us that in their victorious campaign at the Two Rivers in 671, the Northumbrians consisted of a 'little band', while on the other hand the 'bestial Pictish peoples' had 'gathered together innumerable nations from every nook and corner in the north', with the result that the host with which

Ecgfrith was confronted on that occasion was 'enormous' (*inormis*).[11] A certain amount of exaggeration is a given here, with the intention of magnifying the glory of Ecgfrith's victory, yet there is no particular reason to doubt that his expeditionary force was significantly outnumbered in 671. It stands to reason, moreover, that at Dunnichen Ecgfrith was again confronted by a Verturian army significantly larger than his own.

We have seen that Ecgfrith's *exercitus* is likely to have numbered something in the region of 500 or 600 men. Every Anglian figure depicted in the Aberlemno battle-scene is mounted save for the fallen figure at the right of the bottom row, and even he appears to be wearing a hauberk with slits in the skirt to allow for horsemanship; it is on the basis of this evidence that the view has been taken here that, as he had done in 671, the Northumbrian king placed his faith in cavalry alone.[12] For what it is worth, the battle-scene also creates the impression that the Anglians depicted were outnumbered perhaps by as much as three to one. On the whole, then, we might estimate that Bridei's army at Dunnichen consisted of at least 1,000 men, though not more (and probably significantly less) than 2,000 men. In other words, we have good reason to doubt that the forces led to Dunnichen by Ecgfrith and Bridei represented in either case 'the full weight of his military resources'.[13] For Ecgfrith, as has been mentioned already, such factors as mobility, combat experience in Fortriu, and other kinds of familiarity with Bridei and his kingdom may have been overriding ones as he planned his campaign. No doubt throughout such planning he remained mindful at all times of the need not to overcommit himself to a northern war while the Mercians remained a threat. Similarly, the idea that Ecgfrith was opposed by 'a united effort by the Pictish peoples' and 'all the martial power that Pictland could summon together' goes well beyond our evidence.[14] Bridei may not have had the luxury of a great deal of time in order to gather his host, and in any case several prior years of aggressive expansion are likely to have secured for him considerable interests that needed monitoring and protecting from opportunistic enemies. We know nothing about military obligation in Fortriu, but it seems reasonable to presume that, like Ecgfrith's *exercitus*, Bridei's army consisted of his own household warriors and landed retainers, men battle-hardened by recent campaigns as far afield as Orkney and Strathearn. The sword-wielding forward infantry rank in the Aberlemno battle-scene probably represents this element within the Verturian force. Such men will almost certainly have been supported on the day by a body of local levies who were obliged to answer a royal summons to muster in defence of their homeland, since it was probably some prerogative of this kind that had enabled Drust to outnumber an aggressive Ecgfrith so markedly at the Two Rivers. It would have been the presence of this latter group, probably represented by the spear-wielding second and third infantry ranks in the battle-scene, that is likeliest to have tipped the balance of numbers in Bridei's favour.

We will never know whether the size of the Verturian force arranged against Ecgfrith at Dunnichen Hill was masked to a certain extent by woods and other landscape features, or whether he was aware of such dangerously uneven numbers and pressed ahead in spite of the odds as he had done fourteen years earlier. *The Battle of Maldon* suggests the likelihood that the engagement began with an exchange of messages between the royal *fratrueles* offering one another the opportunity to avoid violence. In this later poem, the Danish leaders are said to have sent word to the English ealdorman that:

'You must quickly send gold rings in return for your protection. And it is better for you all that you should buy off this onslaught of spears with tribute-money than that we should join battle so grievously. We need not destroy each other if you are sufficiently wealthy: we are prepared to establish a truce in return for gold. If you who are the richest man here decide that you are willing to ransom your people, willing to give... money in exchange for peace, and to accept protection from us, we are content to embark with the taxes, to set sail across the sea, and to keep the peace with you all.'

This passage is likely to be mostly fanciful, but it seems likely that such formalities were reasonably common in Dark Age insular warfare. If something like it took place on 20 May 685, the subject of the kinship of Ecgfrith and Bridei is almost certain to have been raised. The Northumbrian king may even have employed something of this Danish tactic of attempting to undermine the enemy's resolve to fight by singling out their leader and promising that only he need pay the price of peace.

Clearly any such formal exchange of messages failed to stave off battle at Dunnichen. According to *The Battle of Maldon*, Byrhtnoth responded to his enemies as follows:

'Sea raider, can you hear what this army is saying? They intend to give all of you spears as tribute, deadly points and tried swords… It appears to me too shameful that you should return to your ships with our money unopposed, now that you thus far in this direction have penetrated into our territory. You will not gain treasure so easily: spear and sword must first arbitrate between us, the grim game of battle, before we pay tribute.'[15]

If we accept the present argument that Ecgfrith was no fool, it might be wondered why he would have chosen to press on with the fight when faced with the long odds envisioned here. We cannot, of course, know the answer to this question. It will serve, however, to point out that we need posit neither a Verturian ruse nor an ambush in order to explain how Ecgfrith came to involve himself in battle with an army that proved capable of inflicting such a decisive defeat upon his men. In the first place, it may be pointed out that he seems to have managed spectacularly well the previous time he faced a Verturian army larger than his own in the field, which can only have given heart both to the king himself and also to his men.[16] In addition, we must remain mindful that few honourable alternatives may have been available to Ecgfrith once the size and situation of the army arrayed against him became plain. To illustrate this point, we might recall that, when Ecgfrith was six years old, his father Oswig, at the time king of the Bernicians, took to the field against his wife's kinsman Oswini, king of the Deirans. As Bede recorded:

Each raised an army against his enemy, and Oswini, realising that it was not possible to join war against one who could rely upon greater support, considered it best to give up on the idea of war until more promising times. So he disbanded the army which he had assembled... and he went off with but a single soldier who was faithful to him, named Tondhere, and hid in the house of the *comes* Hunwald, from whom he was accustomed to expect the greatest friendship. But alas and sorrow! It proved otherwise, for he was betrayed by the same *comes* to Oswig, who caused him to be foully slain, together with the aforesaid soldier, by the hand of his *praefectus* Aeðilwini.[17]

Prudence in the face of daunting odds on the battlefield, however admirable it might seem to us, appears to have been interpreted by Hunwald in 651 as shameful cowardice of sufficient magnitude to invalidate his obligation to provide hospitality and security to his king. Such an example from Ecgfrith's youth helps to explain his willingness to risk a fight against superior Pictish numbers at the Two Rivers in 671, as well as why he may have done so again fourteen years later at Dunnichen. As James Campbell has put it, 'men in positions such as those of Oswine or of his men faced horrible dilemmas in which exile or death were often the only ways out'.[18] Having thrown down the gauntlet by invading Fortriu in the first place, Ecgfrith can have had few face-saving options if the tactical situation, having become apparent, caused him any concern.

The anonymous of Lindisfarne, writing some fifteen years after the event, was informed that Ecgfrith had been killed at the ninth hour of the day, which in late May would have been mid- to late afternoon.[19] It was probably not too much earlier than this, then, that the Northumbrian king ordered his horsemen to attack the Verturian position on the lower slopes of Dunnichen Hill. We do not know how the fighting progressed, and can form only very general impressions of how a battle fought under such conditions as those outlined here may have played out, guided to a certain extent by the Aberlemno battle-scene. It has been asserted, presumably as a reading of the images on the battle-scene, that 'the technology… of the Angles was far more advanced than that of the Picts'.[20] One must take great care about applying this idea as a general truism to be applied to Anglian and Pictish society, but the battle-scene does suggest that Ecgfrith and his men were more elaborately equipped than their Verturian opponents at Dunnichen. One might interpret this evidence as indicating that, while Ecgfrith's army consisted primarily of *optimates* and the like who could afford to outfit themselves with the very best weapons and armour, Bridei's consisted primarily of men of lesser station and fewer means.

We have seen various indications that, whereas the successful Roman assault on Calgacus and his men at *Mons Graupius* was led by advancing infantry supported by cavalry, the Northumbrian force at Dunnichen is likely to have consisted mainly, and probably exclusively, of a mounted force (*equitatus exercitus*). The argument that Ecgfrith's expeditionary force, having ridden to the field of battle from their homeland, also fought from horseback as cavalrymen (rather than dismounting to fight as infantry as occurred at Maldon) has withstood recent doubts, largely because of the evidence provided by the Aberlemno battle-scene, which remains forceful even if the likelihood that it commemorates a specific battle like Dunnichen is rejected.[21] The monument depicts the Anglian horsemen in question as having been armed with a targe and a lance – or perhaps a lighter javelin – wielded over the shoulder, and having worn a hauberk with a slit skirt for riding and a helmet with nasal, cheek and neck guards. Faced with a situation of inferior numbers and inferior position, and electing to fight rather than to fly, Agricola's most immediate concern at *Mons Graupius* had been the threat of becoming surrounded, a threat that Ecgfrith too may have faced. To minimise the risk of such a development, the Roman general had 'opened out his ranks' and presented a line that 'looked like being dangerously thin'.[22] We may note at this stage that the middle row of the Aberlemno battle-scene depicts a single Anglian horseman charging into the three ranks of Pictish foot, suggesting that Ecgfrith may well have been of a similar mind at Dunnichen, opening out and thinning his ranks like Agricola in the hopes of staving off any Verturian attempt to surround them. The presence of Restenneth Loch to the left, as well perhaps as the instability of what may have been 'very swampy' loch-side terrain,[23] may be thought to have come into play at this point: Professor Alcock has suggested that it was something like this that exacerbated the Northumbrians' sense of being confined into a narrow space, a key aspect of the battle that was remembered long enough to be preserved by Bede.[24]

The battle of *Mons Graupius* began 'with exchanges of missiles' in which the natives 'rained volleys' upon the Romans from the sloping hillside.[25] There is no indication of Pictish archery in the Aberlemno battle-scene, but the man standing in the third rank in the middle register of the scene is armed with a spear which, in contrast to the man of the second rank, he does not hold at the ready. This might suggest a rank of men held in reserve, except that Cruickshank has pointed out that the spear in question appears to be much lighter than that brandished by the man in front of him,[26] and so may represent some kind of javelin to be thrown at the enemy. *The Battle of Maldon* describes how, as 'the roar of battle was lifted up', the combatants on both sides 'let fly the file-hard spears from their hands then, made fly the fiercely sharpened ones, the darts', and how 'shield absorbed spearhead'.[27] If Ecgfrith and his horsemen had indeed been bottled up to a certain extent and limited in their manoeuvrability by the terrain, they are likely to have been vulnerable to Verturian spears cast from above as they rode towards Bridei's line of infantry and hefted their lances or javelins onto their shoulders. The fact that no Anglian warrior in the Aberlemno battle-scene is depicted as fighting with his sword suggests that the spears depicted here were not javelins to be thrown, but lances (albeit short ones) to be wielded in close-quarters hand-to-hand fighting. It remains a possibility, however, that Ecgfrith's men cast javelins of their own as they bore down upon the Verturian ranks, and thenceforth drew and fought at close quarters with their swords.[28]

The Middle Welsh poem *Gweith Gwen Ystrat*, thought to date from the period contemporary with Dunnichen, speaks of Pictish warriors with 'shrill battle-cries' that were 'like waves across the face of the land'.[29] This, like the reference in *The Battle of Maldon* to 'the roar of battle', allows us to appreciate something of the sounds that were in the ears of Pict and Angle alike at Dunnichen as the fighting commenced. At *Mons Graupius*, the Roman horsemen of Agricola 'plunged into the infantry' arranged against them in a 'terrifying' onslaught.[30] It was probably no less terrifying six centuries later for the men of Fortriu at Dunnichen who bore the brunt of the mounted Northumbrian assault. Small wonder, then, that a depiction of such a coming together of a charging Anglian horseman and three ranks of Pictish infantry braced for the attack occupies the central part of the Aberlemno battle-scene, and that the sculptor envisioned the Anglian horses as large, powerful animals.[31] The monument gives its audience the impression of Pictish swordsmen knocked down by charging horses or run through by lances and of Anglian horsemen and their mounts bloodied by spiked shield-bosses and laid low by swords, javelins and heavy spears. The upper register of the scene seems to show Pictish weapons strewn on the field of battle and an Anglian horseman having commandeered a Pictish mount,[32] reminding the audience that, whatever the ultimate results of the battle, the Northumbrian onslaught is likely to have been fierce, and to have resulted in a number of Verturian casualties.

Agricola had deployed his cavalry as support for his infantry at *Mons Graupius*; even so the Roman advance was ground to a standstill on the one hand by 'the solid ranks of the enemy' who stood their ground and on the other by 'the roughness of the ground'.[33] We have already seen indications that Bridei too may have benefited from both of these tactical advantages provided that his men, like those of Calgacus, stood their ground and did not break ranks when Ecgfrith sent his horsemen thundering into the Verturian infantry positions. The Northumbrians, lacking the infantry support enjoyed by Agricola, would probably have found the idea of such a sustained assault much less attractive. Ecgfrith may have elected to take fuller advantage of the mounted mobility of his men by employing hit-and-run tactics, striking as effectively as could be managed and then withdrawing before the men of Fortriu had the chance to surround or unhorse their opponents. Such a scenario would allow the battle of Dunnichen to have lasted for some time as Ecgfrith sent wave after wave of horsemen against ranked Verturian infantry who weathered each onslaught and regrouped to bear the brunt of the next attack. This appears to be the kind of thing described in *Gweith Gwen Ystrat*, where the poet seems to envision British warriors who 'stood their ground' throughout fighting that took up a morning.[34] It is equally possible, however, that Ecgfrith, weighing his options and sizing up his enemy, staked all on one great cavalry charge with the intention of breaking through the Verturian ranks to deal directly with Bridei, trusting in the mobility of his forces to save them if things went awry. In that event the battle of Dunnichen may have been a relatively short-lived encounter, and it would seem likely that in such an attack the Northumbrians would have been more readily brought to a halt than Agricola's infantry-led advance had been at *Mons Graupius*.

If indeed Ecgfrith elected to risk all in this way, he stood to lose all if his enemy failed to break ranks and run. Tacitus relates that, as the Roman cavalry charge came to nothing because the native forces held their ground,

Calgacus took the initiative. The natives 'on the hilltops' (who 'had so far taken no part in the action and had leisure to note with contempt the smallness of our numbers') began 'to descend gradually' upon the Romans in an attempt 'to envelop our victorious rear' by virtue of pure numerical advantage.[35] Had Calgacus been more fortunate, this might have proven to be the turning point in the battle of *Mons Graupius*. As things turned out, however, Agricola, through the timely deployment of his reserve cavalry, was successful on that occasion in turning 'their spirited charge into a disorderly rout'.[36] Thus did the Romans secure victory at *Mons Graupius*, but it may well have been a timely Verturian counter-attack of a similar nature that led to the Northumbrian defeat at Dunnichen and the routing of Ecgfrith's forces. *Gweith Gwen Ystrat*, too, seems to speak of similarly separate phases of the battle it purports to describe. At first the British force stands its ground against a Pictish one; then it mounts some form of counter-attack with 'a fierce and energetic cry', driving the enemy against a river, while 'one could see a constricted barrier of laureate champions forced to a standstill'.[37] We may certainly note, following Cruickshank, that the three ranks of Pictish infantry depicted in the middle register of the Aberlemno battle-scene appear to be engaged in 'a walking motion', suggesting some kind of advance, perhaps (but not necessarily) 'in closed-rank formation'.[38]

If Bridei was confronted with hit-and-run tactics and a more lengthy fight, he may have initiated such an advance at a critical point – perhaps at a moment when the Northumbrians seemed disorganised or dispirited, or after they seemed to have suffered a requisite number of casualties or to have exhausted themselves or their horses. On the other hand, if the battle was short and consisted of a single Northumbrian charge, it is likely to have been at the point at which this assault had petered out that the Verturian king mounted a counter-attack. At some point, having been bested on the field, Ecgfrith will have attempted an orderly withdrawal, disorganised flight, or something in between. It was no doubt at this point that *Linn Garan* became such an important factor that it went on to lend its name to the battle in the reckoning of both the Verturian and the Anglian (*Nechtanesmere*) protagonists. This is most readily explained by the presumption that a significant number of the Northumbrian dead met their end in the waters of this 'crane lake' which we have been identifying as the early historic version of Restenneth Loch. A parallel may be drawn here with the number of Picts who were drowned at the Two Rivers in 671, giving rise to the image of rivers so choked with the Pictish dead that Northumbrian warriors could pass dry-foot over them.[39]

In the upper register of the Aberlemno battle-scene we find depicted an Anglian horseman, apparently mounted upon a Pictish horse, who appears to be in flight from a sword-wielding Pictish horseman behind him.[40] Similarly, in the lower register of the scene, we find depicted two horsemen, one Pictish and the other Anglian, locked in combat with one another with their spears. These images clearly suggest that Verturian horsemen armed with a targe, a sword and a spear were involved in the battle of Dunnichen, in some cases fighting with their Anglian counterparts and in others chasing after those who had fled. The implications of this evidence are that Bridei, in addition to arranging the main body of his men as infantry in the manner outlined here, had at his disposal a body of horsemen which would seem to have played a crucial role in the fighting at the point when the Northumbrians endeavoured to make their escape from the battlefield. A scenario that offers itself, accounting both for the involvement in the battle of Restenneth Loch and for the likelihood that Ecgfrith and the majority of his men were denied the opportunity to escape from the field with their lives, would be that the Verturian king, at an opportune moment, deployed a detachment of his horse to descend from Green Hill and ride out westwards with the intention of blocking the Northumbrian line of retreat towards the high ground separating the Loch of Forfar from Restenneth Loch. If, as proposed here, Bridei ordered his infantry forward from their positions at a timely moment, it may well have been at about this same time that he sent his cavalry forth to deny the enemy an easy escape.

In such a scenario the Northumbrians will have been confronted by the sight of a mass of Verturian spear-men advancing down the slopes of Green Hill and a sortie of Bridei's horsemen riding west to their right in an attempt to cut off their intended line of retreat. Having made up their mind to withdraw, Ecgfrith's men will have had little option but to veer off northwards in the direction of Restenneth Loch, hoping perhaps to outflank or outmanoeuvre the Verturian cavalry in order to reach the high ground at Forfar ahead of them. A horseman at full rein will very shortly, however, have had wet ground to contend with and then Restenneth Loch itself alongside or in front of him. We get a vivid picture of this terrible phase of battle from Tacitus, who says that, among the defeated natives at *Mons Graupius*:

> each man now behaved according to his character. Whole groups, though they had weapons in their hands, fled before inferior numbers; elsewhere, unarmed men deliberately charged to face certain death. Equipment, bodies, and mangled limbs lay all around on the bloodstained earth; and even the vanquished now and then recovered their fury and their courage… At length, when they saw our troops re-formed and steady, renewing the pursuit, they turned and ran. They no longer kept formation or looked to see where their comrades were, but scattering and deliberately keeping apart from each other they penetrated far into trackless wilds.[41]

Some of Ecgfrith's men chose in their panic to surrender.[42] *Gweith Gwen Ystrat*, describing a Pictish force hemmed against a river by their British adversaries, speaks of 'bloodstained men' with their 'arms relinquished before the hoary ruler' of the Britons, who 'wanted peace because they had fought to exhaustion' and were gathered up 'shivering on the gravel bank' where 'their centurions were counted up according to seniority'.[43] Others among the retreating Northumbrian expeditionary force would seem to have taken their chances with the waters of *Linn Garan* that lay between themselves and escape. Again, *Gweith Gwen Ystrat* says of Pictish fugitives from that encounter that 'waves washed the manes of their horses'.[44] Restenneth Loch must have claimed a considerable number of lives that day, as men and horses wearied by battle, weighed down by armour and equipment, and panicked by their danger plunged into the water in what for many proved a vain hope of escape.

If, as has been suggested here, Bridei did not deploy his cavalry until some decisive moment, the Aberlemno battle-scene suggests that some of the Anglian horsemen, represented in its lower register, elected to try to fight their way through the advancing Verturian horse to safety. Bede was under the impression that 'the king, his bodyguard slain around him, was laid low by the sword of an enemy',[45] and it is interesting that *Iniu feras Bruide cath* also speaks of Ecgfrith having been 'slain in battle against iron swords'.[46] It is very difficult to assess the quality of such information as proof of the actual events surrounding the killing of the king. Professor Alcock has argued that 'anyone close enough to the king to observe the sequence of deaths would, by that very fact, have had a low expectation of life'.[47] This may be an excessively Anglo-centric view, however, since we must assume that there were Picts near at hand when Ecgfrith fell who survived to relate the details of what they had witnessed. We cannot dismiss out of hand the possibility that some Verturian account of the battle, perhaps a heroic poem or a 'song of victory',[48] provided the basis for the information conveyed both to Bede and to the Gaelic poet about the king's death, suitably framed in the former instance by the image of a fallen bodyguard. On the other hand, we can hardly be certain that Ecgfrith made a last stand of this kind and fell locked in combat alongside his *optimates*, although it may well be true.

The Battle of Maldon gives the impression that leaders

like Ecgfrith were liable to attract a great deal of attention
from their enemies in a battle situation. A man like
Ecgfrith secured and maintained his royal position in part
because he was a formidable warrior, but for many the
rewards of killing such a man must have outweighed the
risks of fighting him. He who had slain a king might, for
example, take the opportunity to relieve the body of such
things as 'arm-rings, the robe and gold bands, and the
ornamented sword', while at the same time increasing his
reputation and striking a decisive blow that might well
turn the tide of battle, since the discipline of a Dark Age
warband seems commonly to have disintegrated upon the
death of its leader.[49] Ecgfrith, then, may have been killed
relatively early in the battle as a result of a Pictish javelin,
or in the carnage of the main fighting below Green Hill.
Alternatively, the king and his bodyguard may have survived
long enough to see the turning of the tide of battle against
them, only to fall in their attempt to escape the field. In
fact, we are guided both by our literary sources and by the
Aberlemno battle-scene in the direction of this last option
– that Ecgfrith and his *optimates* were among those who
chose in the latter stages of the battle to fight their way
to safety. The literary testimony already discussed aside, it
is in the lower register of the scene – where an Anglian
horseman is depicted fighting his Pictish adversary – and
not in the upper one, where the Anglian horseman is in
flight, that the sculptor elected to place the evocative figure
of a slain Anglian warrior. His shield lies beside him and
a carrion bird is at his throat. Cruickshank has drawn our
attention both to the fact that this figure is 'unnaturally
large' in comparison with the other human figures in the

battle-scene and to the likelihood that this indicates the 'particular importance' of the man being represented. There can be little doubt that he has correctly identified this figure as depicting Ecgfrith himself.[50]

The Battle of Maldon provides an example, if a fanciful one, of the range of effects that the death of a leader might have upon his army. On the one hand, the poet lists those who shamefully ran away; on the other he enthusiastically describes how others who might also have escaped 'pushed on eagerly', intending 'to lose their lives or to avenge their friend', with the result in each case that 'he lay near his lord as a thegn should'.[51] Bede reports that by the end of the battle of Dunnichen many of his fellow Northumbrians had been 'either slain by the sword or taken into servitude', while others had 'escaped by flight from the land of the Picts'.[52] There is every reason to believe that it was in the final phase of the engagement that most of those who died – being 'the greater part of the forces he [Ecgfrith] had taken with him'[53] – lost their lives. A large proportion of the slain must have been claimed by *Linn Garan*. It seems to have been much the same at the battle of the Two Rivers in 671, where Ecgfrith and his warriors, having defeated their Pictish opponents, then 'pursued and slew a crowd of fugitives'.[54] In the case of Dunnichen we lack such detail, and have nothing to match Tacitus's account of how at *Mons Graupius* the victorious Roman general 'ordered strong cohorts of light infantry to ring the woods' into which his opponents had fled, scouring the woods with cavalry and 'dismounted troopers' and ensuring that 'the pursuit went on until night fell and our soldiers were tired of killing'.[55] There is an echo of this in *Gweith Gwen*

Ystrat, in which the poet says that, upon the conclusion of the fighting, 'I saw… a mustering, re-sharpened and severe for battle', and that 'it was not flight that the battle-protector contemplated' but pursuit, noting that 'neither open plain nor woods gave shelter to your oppressors, O protector of the folk, when they arrived'.[56] The aftermath of Dunnichen, obscure though it is, is very likely to have been as ugly and as murderous as the final phase of these other engagements. If such bloodlust is only to be expected as a consequence of war, it is notable at least that the victorious men of Fortriu evidently exercised a modicum of restraint amid this carnage, taking some of their vanquished foes into custody.[57]

The foregoing reconstruction of the main action of the afternoon of 20 May 685 has been of necessity composed of hypothesis and speculation based upon a number of key assumptions. Though it is also informed throughout by the impressionistic nature of our meagre sources, there remains, as there must, much scope for disagreement and debate. One cannot hope to be conclusive in this matter, and can strive only to offer a scenario which is plausible and faithful to the evidence, seeking at all times to avoid the entirely fanciful. In the final analysis there are few things about which we can be certain with regard to the battle of Dunnichen. There can be little doubt of the violence of the engagement, whether it was a protracted affair or a quick and decisive clash of arms. Neither is there much room for doubt about the devastating death-toll on the Northumbrian side, although we need not go so far as to suggest that 'of the survivors, of which there were not many, most were enslaved by the Picts', nor that 'only a few struggled back home to break the awesome news to their people'.[58] The idea that Ecgfrith's army was 'annihilated' would seem to be an extreme reading of Bede.[59] He does not say that there were not many survivors – only that their number was less than the number of the slain – and there is little in his statement that 'many of the Anglian nation were either slain by the sword or taken into servitude or escaped by flight from the land of the Picts' that invites us to give more priority to the number of men captured than to the number who escaped.[60]

1 Aberlemno battle-scene.

2 Aberlemno kirkyard cross-slab, the obverse side; the battle-scene is on the reverse side. The cross is carved in stunningly high relief.

3 Bamburgh; the Bernician stronghold of *Bebbanburg* on this rock was the chief royal centre of Ecgfrith's kingdom.

4 Dumbarton; the British stronghold of *Al Clut* on this rock was the main royal centre of the kingdom ruled by Bridei's father Beli.

5 Dunnottar; the Pictish stronghold of *Dún Foither* on this rock was besieged in 680, probably by Bridei.

6 Abercorn; the Bernician monastery of *Aebbercurnig* on this spot became an episcopal seat in 681, with jurisdiction over the *prouincia Pictorum*.

7 Doon Hill above Dunbar; the Bernician stronghold of *Dynbaer* served as a prison for St Wilfrith, and may have hosted Ecgfrith on his final campaign.

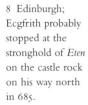

8 Edinburgh; Ecgfrith probably stopped at the stronghold of *Eten* on the castle rock on his way north in 685.

9 Stirling Castle (in the distance to the left); the stronghold of *Iudeu* on this rock stood guard over the lowest crossing-place of the River Forth.

10 Stirling Bridge; Ecgfrith will have crossed the Forth at the sight of the old bridge (of William Wallace fame), which stood to the left of the present one.

11 Strathearn; the view eastwards from Dunning Hill. It was probably here that Ecgfrith began plundering Verturian farms.

12 Moncrieffe Hill; the Verturian stronghold of *Monid Chroib* stood upon the bare summit of the hill visible in the centre of the photograph.

13 Moncrieffe Hill; on the site of *Monid Chroib*.

14 Abernethy; the Rivers Earn and Tay in the background. The round tower marks the site of the monastery, the seat of the bishop of Fortriu.

15 Strathmore; viewed from Kemp's Castle. The loch in the middle of the photograph is the Loch of Forfar.

16 Dunnichen Hill; as viewed from Kemp's Castle to the north. The two hills are separated by Rescobie Loch, which in 685 formed part of Restenneth Loch.

17 Kemp's Castle; on the summit of Turin Hill. It is possible that this was the most important royal centre in Fortriu until the time of Bridei.

18 Dunnichen Hill from the north-east. The traditional battlefield site alongside Dunnichen Moss lies on the sloping ground to the left of the hill.

19 The battle monument erected in the village of Dunnichen in commemoration of the thirteenth centenary of the battle. In the background is Dunnichen Moss.

20 The remains of Dunnichen Moss; drained almost entirely in the eighteenth century. At its height the water will have filled much of this hollow.

21 Dunnichen Battlefield (as understood here); viewed from Kemp's Castle. Restenneth Loch reached from Rescobie Loch on the left to Loch Fithie in the centre and as far to the right as the clumps of trees in the middle distance at the end of the ridge from which the photograph was taken. Bridei probably deployed his men beyond this loch on the lower slopes of Dunnichen Hill on the left of the photograph. Ecgfrith approached from the right.

22 Dunnichen Hill viewed through the trees from Restenneth Priory. The reedy plants in the foreground mark the former Restenneth Loch.

23 Turin Hill in the further distance; viewed from Restenneth Priory. The hollow down the slope here was formerly submerged within Restenneth Loch.

24 The lower slopes of the west side of Dunnichen Hill; the summit is marked by a mast. Bridei is understood here to have deployed his men hereabouts.

25 Dunnichen battlefield (as understood here); viewed from the south with Turin Hill in the background just to the right of centre. Dunnichen Hill lies to the right of shot, and Restenneth Loch will have lain in the middle distance.

26 Dunnichen battlefield (as understood here); viewed from the south-east. Restenneth Priory, marking the westernmost extent of Restenneth Loch, lies behind the trees in the middle distance.

27 Dunnichen battlefield (as understood here); viewed from the east towards the higher ground over which Ecgfrith approached Dunnichen Hill.

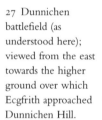

28 The lower slopes of the west side of Dunnichen Hill; the summit is to the right, marked by its mast.

29 Pictish footmen in the middle register of the Aberlemno battle-scene.

Above: 30 Anglian horseman attacking Pictish footmen in the middle register of the Aberlemno battle-scene.

Right: 31 Aberlemno battle-scene, the upper register.

Above: 32 Aberlemno battle-scene, the lower register.

Left: 33 Slain Anglian warrior in the lower register of the Aberlemno battle-scene. This, in all likelihood, is a representation of Ecgfrith.

Opposite, top: 34 Inchcolm Priory in the Firth of Forth. It is possible that Ecgfrith was buried on this island rather than on Iona.

Opposite, middle: 35 Restenneth Priory on its promontory; in 685 this spot was almost surrounded by Restenneth Loch. Dunnichen Hill stands in the background; the battlefield lies beyond the trees to the right, no longer visible from this spot due to the presence of a quarry.

Opposite, bottom: 36 Aberlemno kirk lies in the centre of the photograph, viewed from Kemp's Castle on Turin Hill.

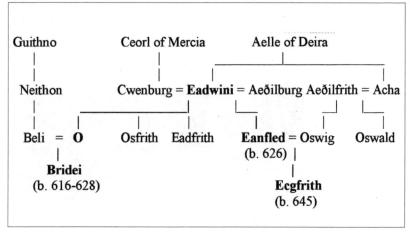

37 *Fratrueles*: ties of kinship between Bridei f. Beli and Ecgfrith son of Oswig.

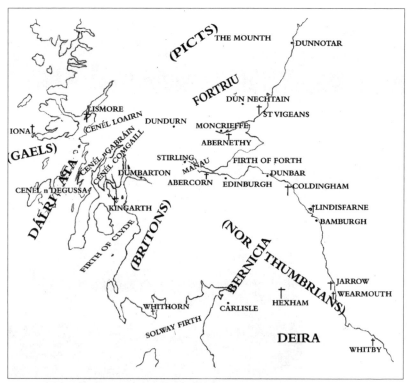

38 Northern Britain in the time of Ecgfrith and Bridei.

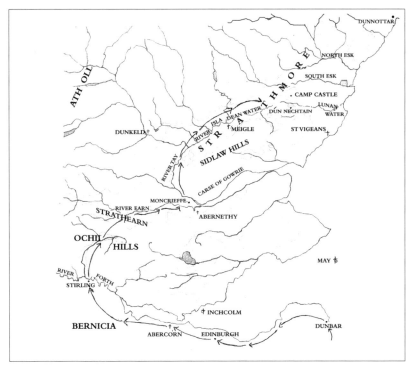

39 The course of Ecgfrith's invasion of Fortriu (conjectural).

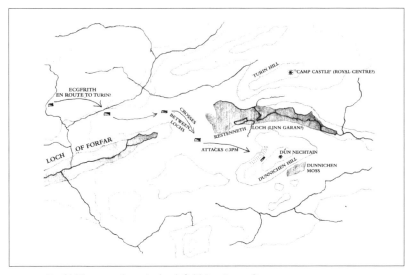

40 Ecgfrith's approach to the battlefield (conjectural).

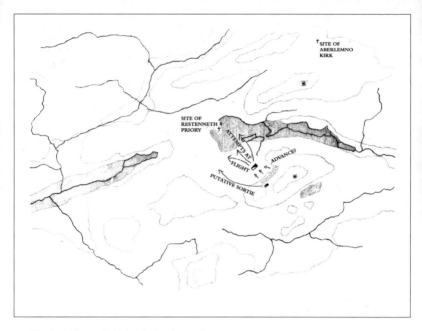

41 The final phase of the battle (conjectural).

6

In the Wake of
'Ecgfrith's Battle'

The sensational news of the outcome of the battle of
Dunnichen spread quickly throughout Britain and Ireland.
Ecgfrith had been a key figure in insular politics and
Anglo-Saxon ecclesiastical affairs, and it must have been
with a fair degree of shock and disbelief that word of
his death at the hands of the Verturian Picts was received
across the insular zone. Never before had an Anglian king
fallen in battle against an army of northern natives, and the
episode would prove quite unique in British history. The
news made sufficient impact to allow the contemporary
abbot of Iona to feel comfortable more than a decade
later in using 'Ecgfrith's battle' (*bellum Ecfridi*) as a point
of reference for dating in a work that was written with a
pan-insular, and perhaps even wider, audience in mind.[1]
Bede alleges that word of the death of the king reached his
second wife Iurminburg and Cuthbert at Carlisle (*Luel*), in
the latter's see of Hexham, on Monday 22 May through
'one who had fled from the fight', a man who must have

ridden his horse very hard.[2] It cannot have reached the main Bernician royal stronghold at Bamburgh much later than this. 'After a few days', according to the anonymous of Lindisfarne, the news 'had been announced far and wide that a wretched and mournful battle had taken place'.[3] Against all expectations the king had been slain far from home by his own *fratruelis* and erstwhile subordinate, and even among the supporters of the exiled Bishop Wilfrith, whose inability to get along with Ecgfrith proved to be the ruin of his career, his death alongside so many of his men was considered 'a most woeful disaster'.[4]

Some of the first questions to arise at Bamburgh must have surrounded the fate of the royal remains. Had his body been recovered by his own men, as seems to have been the case when Aelfwini was killed at the Trent in 679, it seems very likely that the Deiran monastery of Whitby (*Streanaeshelch*) in North Yorkshire would have been chosen as the final resting place of Ecgfrith son of Oswig. He had, after all, seen to it that his father was buried there in 670, and this prominent monastery was to develop further as a royal burial ground in the years to come when his mother Eanfled and her father Eadwini became interred there as well.[5] We do not know where his brother Aelfwini was buried in 679, nor his successor Aldfrith 'who was said to be the son of his father' Oswig in 705,[6] but entombment alongside the other members of the Oswegian royal family at Whitby must surely top any list of likelihoods. It seems on the whole much more in keeping with the circumstances of the battle of Dunnichen, however, to presume that the king's remains were not recovered by his countrymen as they fled the battlefield. His body may indeed have lain for some time between the hill and Forfar before pains were taken by the victorious men of Fortriu to identify and make provision for the Anglian dead. Bede provides us with an interesting contemporary glimpse of just this kind of thing in his story of Imma, a Deiran warrior who fought for Ecgfrith and Aelfwini at the Trent in 679 and was stricken down there, although he was only injured. This man, according to Bede's source, 'lay all that day and the following night amongst the bodies of the slain as though dead, but at last he recovered consciousness' and attempted to make his way from the battlefield.[7]

The battle of Dunnichen was fought in the mid-afternoon, and the pursuit of Northumbrian fugitives by Bridei's men probably went on until nightfall – which on 20 May comes late in northern Britain. Here too, then, the slain and the dying may well have lain strewn about the field or undisturbed in the waters of *Linn Garan* until the next morning at least. It is also entirely possible that his enemies did not initially note the death of Ecgfrith unless he stood out markedly from his bodyguard. Hand-to-hand fighting is a grisly and distracting business. The Scottish king James IV famously was not known to have been killed at Flodden in 1513 until his plundered body was discovered and identified among the slain when the field was being picked over.[8] Bede tells us that Imma's own brother misidentified someone else's battered remains as those of Imma himself,[9] and it may have been some time before the body of the slain Northumbrian king was discovered, identified and recovered from the battlefield below Dunnichen Hill. Others who had fought in

Ecgfrith's expeditionary force may have shared the fate of Imma, who, having been incapacitated and discovered alive among the slain on the day after the battle of the Trent, had his wounds seen to by his enemies, who ensured that he was 'bound at night to prevent his escape' and eventually sold him into captivity.[10]

It is generally accepted that the remains of Ecgfrith, having been recovered from the battlefield (probably some time on Sunday 21 May), were then conveyed rather extraordinarily to the island of Iona where the king was thought to have been laid to rest. As it stands this tradition is no older than the comparatively late testimony of Simeon of Durham, who recorded in the twelfth century, no doubt from an earlier source, that the king's remains were 'buried on Iona, the island of Columba' (*in Hii, insula Columbae*).[11] In a different study the present writer has spelled out at some length the reasons for doubting that Bridei map Beli, despite the testimony of one later source, is likely to have had any particular predilections towards Iona or the Columban *familia*. This is not the place to rehearse this evidence; for the present purposes it will suffice to point out that a case can be made for believing that Iona emerged as a powerful force in Verturian ecclesiastical affairs only in the generation after the death of the victor of Dunnichen. For this reason there is room for doubt as to whether Bridei had any spiritual reason to arrange for the transportation of the body of his *fratruelis* to Iona for burial.[12] The same clearly cannot be said, however, of Ecgfrith's successor Aldfrith, who before he acquired the kingship had been a monk on Iona and can conceivably have had his reasons for desiring the burial of his predecessor on the island. Alternatively, it may be thought possible that Bridei went to Iona in search of Aldfrith as soon as he knew that Ecgfrith had been killed, and that he brought the king's body with him on this journey. Such a hypothesis would, however, require us to believe that the Verturian king was more aware than Ecgfrith's own sister of the existence of Aldfrith and of his alleged viability as heir to the kingdom of his dead *fratruelis*. In addition, both Bede and *Iniu feras Bruide cath* suggest that the resentment aroused by Berct's expedition in 684 ran deep among the Uí Néill in Meath. In that event it must be thought fairly unlikely that Adomnán, the abbot of Iona and a man of Uí Néill descent himself who is likely to have looked upon Berct's victims with considerable sympathy as his kinsmen, would have welcomed the burial of the architect of their suffering on Iona. St Colum Cille had also, after all, been a member of the Uí Néill, and it is difficult to rationalise any decision on Adomnán's part to allow such a burial, save perhaps as a major gesture to Aldfrith.

Though it is clearly not utterly inexplicable, there is nevertheless an air of unlikelihood about the idea that Ecgfrith was interred on Iona. Interestingly, however, there was another island that was probably called *insula Columbae* ('island of Columba') in Latin in the time of Ecgfrith and which, being much more proximate geographically to Dún Nechtain and Fortriu, may be thought as having potentially been the burial place of Ecgfrith. The island in question is Inchcolm in the Firth of Forth (the Gaelic place-name means 'island of Colum'), which lies therefore in what has been construed here as having been frontier territory inhabited by Picts but controlled by Ecgfrith until his death. A contemporary church situated on this island would have been administered by Trumwini as part of his see based at Abercorn further up the firth. If we may accept in principle the possibility that some later scribe – perhaps Simeon himself, who was by all indications a Columban aficionado – mistook an existing early reference to the interment of Ecgfrith upon *insula Columbae* as indicating the most famous island of this name rather than a lesser one like Inchcolm, there is at least a possibility that it was to Inchcolm and not to Iona that Bridei conveyed the body of his fallen *fratruelis* in the days after Dunnichen. It is also possible, given the remarkable fact that within a century of his death Ecgfrith (to the horror of Reeves) was commemorated by the Irish as a saint, that his feast day on 27 May marks the burial ('translation') of the king seven days after he was killed, in which case the Iona tradition would have to be rejected.[13] It is certainly fairly straightforward to appreciate the symbolism of political change that would have been apparent to Verturian observers in Gowrie and the Picts of the frontier territory to the south as the body of the slain Northumbrian over-king was processed southwards on its final journey. Probably nothing short of the discovery of Ecgfrith's tomb (a highly unlikely development) somewhere other than Iona is likely to undermine the powerful tradition of his Ionan burial, but it is not impossible that he was actually buried much closer to home – within sight, indeed, of Bernician Lothian. If nothing else we may suspect that Bridei came south soon after his victory to dismiss Trumwini as bishop of the *prouincia Pictorum*, at which point the latter, according to Bede, 'retired with his companions from the monastery… commended his own people to his friends in such monasteries as he could find and chose his own place of retirement' in the monastery of Whitby.[14]

Predictably, and as we have already seen, the tragedy of the king's death was to become interpreted by various Northumbrian commentators as having come about 'in accordance with the predestined judgement of God'. Ecgfrith's motives in making war upon the king of Fortriu were forgotten in a frenzy of moralistic rationalisation. Supporters of Wilfrith came to the decision that the king had sealed his fate as a result of his expulsion of their hero from his episcopate in 678.[15] Others adopted the decidedly Gaelic perspective that understood the outcome of the battle of Dunnichen as having been the inevitable result of Berct's expedition to Meath in 684. Bede, writing with the hindsight of half a century, famously wrote in addition that from the time of the battle of Dunnichen, 'the hopes and strength of the Anglian kingdom began to ebb and fall away'. Not only was it the case that the men of Fortriu 'recovered their own land which the Angles had held', probably, as we have seen, along the Forth frontier, but their victory had also undermined the Northumbrian capacity to maintain *imperium* in other parts of northern Britain, such that 'the Gaels who were in Britain and some part of the Britons recovered their liberty'.[16] It was not every historical development that motivated the great scholar of Jarrow to quote from Vergil,[17] and we can only surmise that in Bede's opinion the death of Ecgfrith on 20 May 685 was an event of some significance. Most students of this period, and those of the battle in particular, have been inclined to follow Bede on this point. The result has been that Bridei's victory over his *fratruelis* is commonly cast as the single greatest turning point in the history of the Northumbrian kingdom, sealing its fate as a region doomed to be broken by Scandinavian aggression and subsumed by southern English kings.

Hindsight of a slightly different kind has also dominated assessments of the significance of the battle of Dunnichen when examined from the Verturian perspective. It has now been more than half a century since Wainwright's perceptive complaint that:

> to say that the north would have become an Anglian province if Ecgfrith had won… is less accurate than to say that the north might have become part of the Northumbrian kingdom if Ecgfrith and the Northumbrians had had sufficient strength to meet and defeat the Pictish hosts in hostile territory and far from their own bases.[18]

All these years later, however, the view that Bridei's victory at Dunnichen was 'vital for the future nationhood of Scotland' is alive and well, persisting in much of the most recent historiography on the topic.[19] The assumptions underlying such a view are many and varied. It may also be pointed out that, in the wake of Wainwright's work, the persistence of this one-dimensional interpretation of the battle's significance can only be seen as wilful – so much so that it becomes difficult not to be cynical about the different motives that have sustained it. In recent times romanticised assessments of the background and significance of the battle have been driven to a certain extent by a desire to situate it in the 'front garden' of Scottish history,[20] attempting to maximise its public profile in the interests of attracting attention to thirteen-hundredth anniversary celebrations in 1985. In the absence of any comprehensive modern study such work has been far better than nothing, and may well have been absolutely crucial in providing support to those whose tireless efforts have succeeded so far in preserving Dunnichen Hill from quarrying. Such constructive effects aside, however, it must be doubted whether the argument that, insofar as it contributed to 'the ending of Northumbrian expansion northwards', the battle of Dunnichen was 'an important event for the development of the Scottish nation' is a sustainable one.[21]

In addition to needlessly sidelining centuries of complex subsequent political and cultural history, such a perspective on Bridei's victory, by suggesting that the Scottish nation cannot have formed if northern Britain had been anglicised by the Bernicians, perpetuates tired preconceptions regarding the relative degrees of Scottishness that may be assigned arbitrarily to the Celtic and Anglian denizens of what is now eastern Scotland. Similarly, while nationalist sentiment in Scotland might find appealing the notion that the men of Fortriu, prefiguring the days of Wallace and Bruce, single-handedly 'reversed the tide of Northumbrian expansion for ever',[22] it is inescapable that much of the reason for the permanence of the contraction of Northumbrian ambition noted by Bede had little to do with the grim events of 20 May 685. There can be little doubt that the contraction of Ecgfrith's *imperium* after Dunnichen left to Aldfrith and his successors only a fraction of the total amount of tribute that had once provided Oswig and Ecgfrith with the resources to extend their influence over their neighbours.[23] The modern student of the battle of Dunnichen must not, however, be tempted to follow Bede in his decision to ignore the severity and significance of the blow struck against the Northumbrians by Aeðilred on the Trent six years before Dunnichen. It had, after all, been their relationship with the Mercians, and not their dealings with Fortriu, that had dominated the foreign affairs of Ecgfrith's predecessors and people throughout the seventh century. The capacity of Aldfrith and his successors to spend prolonged periods of time away from home in order to make war upon their northern neighbours cannot have been unaffected by the looming and proximate threat of the Mercians and the hegemony constructed by their kings in the century and more after Aeðilred's victory. Indeed, it must be suspected that the rise of Mercia was the primary factor in undermining most of the more aggressive former aspects of Northumbrian policy.

Similarly, without specific knowledge of the size of Ecgfrith's expeditionary force as compared with other seventh-century examples we have very little grounds for assuming that at Dunnichen 'Northumbria suffered her most grievous defeat'.[24] It is a fact which does not excessively belittle the magnitude of the event that the death of Ecgfrith marked the fourth time in three generations that a seventh-century king of both Bernicia and Deira had been decisively defeated and slain in battle. On two of these occasions – after the deaths of Eadwini in 633 and Oswald in 642 – the Northumbrian kingdoms appear to have been placed under tribute, thereafter suffering from the sometimes repeated depredations of their victorious enemies. The battle of Dunnichen, though understandably viewed at the time as a tragic development, apparently brought with it no such consequences. Neither was it 'the flower of Northumbria',[25] according to Bede, who fell at Dunnichen, but the flower of the force that the king had brought with him, prompting the anonymous of Lindisfarne to lament 'the fall of the members of the royal house by a cruel hand and a hostile sword'.[26] The number and social status of those slain with Ecgfrith may not have been any greater than had been the case among those who died with Eadwini much closer to home at Hatfield Chase or on campaign with Oswald in Shropshire, or even indeed on the Trent with Aelfwini only six years earlier.

Upon a full examination of the evidence the present writer is persuaded, as Wainwright pointed out some time ago, that, with regard to 'finally halting the Anglo-Saxon advance into northern Britain' and the decline and ultimate collapse of the Northumbrian kingdom,[27] the battle of Dunnichen was 'an illustration rather than a cause' of the forces involved.[28] Even constrained within narrower limits, eighth-century Northumbria remained a vibrant cultural force within the insular zone for generations after the death of Ecgfrith, and mighty enough even in the throes of political instability to preserve extensive borders against the turned tables of Mercian and Verturian aggression.[29] With even greater hindsight than Bede (although the date of its British source may well have been relatively early), the History of the Britons records of the battle of Dunnichen that 'the Saxon thugs never increased thence to exact tribute from the Picts'.[30] This would seem to be true, as far as we can tell from contemporary evidence, but it is no less significant that the fifty years between the deaths of Ecgfrith and Bede witnessed two more significant conflicts between the men of Fortriu and the Northumbrians. In 698 and in 711 first the former and then the latter secured seemingly decisive victory in these clashes, both of which may well have involved numbers of men comparable to the battle of Dunnichen.[31] We know very little about the circumstances surrounding either of these later campaigns save for the names of some key figures slain in them, but it would seem presumptuous indeed to assume that Bridei's victory in 685 'meant a permanent end to Northumbrian pretensions of overlordship north of the Forth'.[32] The contemporary evidence indicates instead that few Verturian or Anglian prognosticators in the time of Bede will have been so bold as to forecast that Fortriu would remain thereafter beyond the reach of 'the Saxon thugs' (or indeed *vice versa*). The events of 20 May 685 had probably not robbed the Northumbrians of either the ability or the willingness to take up arms in aggression against their Verturian neighbours, and Bede himself ventured to say only that 'at this time the Pictish nation has a treaty of peace with the Anglian nation'.[33] The future of this arrangement was anyone's guess, and Bede made no predictions.

If there is little evidence that the battle of Dunnichen was the beginning of the end of the kingdom of Northumbria, the premature death of Ecgfrith might arguably be seen as the beginning of the end nevertheless of the royal Bernician dynasty established by Aeðilfrith his grandfather.[34] These 'Aeðilfrithings' had dominated the affairs of the northern Anglo-Saxon zone and the neighbouring Celtic regions for something like a century before the demise of the dynasty in the early eighth century. Though he had married twice Ecgfrith died childless at the age of forty. The succession of Aldfrith, whose Aeðilfrithing heritage, as has been mentioned, was evidently open to considerable question, bears all the hallmarks of scraping the bottom of the dynastic barrel in the search for any viable heir. Within another generation Aldfrith's son Osred had been assassinated and the dynasty had failed. There followed a period of political instability as rival claimants to the kingship only distantly related to Ecgfrith vied with one another, a situation that can only have further undermined their capacity to expand their northern interests at the expense of such neighbours as the Verturian hegemony.[35] It is perhaps in this regard that the outcome of the battle of Dunnichen might be construed as having had its most significant effects upon the future of the Northumbrian kingdom, yet even here it must be conceded that such influence was indirect at best, and that other factors and historical accidents had their part to play in bringing about the unstable political atmosphere within which Bede lived out his adult life.

To appraise the significance of the battle of Dunnichen with a view only to its effects, real or imagined, upon Northumbria, however, strikes the present writer as remarkably Anglo-centric. It is not an unassailable position that the outcome of Ecgfrith's campaign meant that 'all the incursions of the Northumbrians [into Fortriu], effected during the previous thirty years by dynastic, political and military means, were brought to nought',[36] for we have seen that, on the contrary, it is possible that Anglian influences in Fortriu during the time of Oswig and Ecgfrith were instrumental in bringing Bridei to power and in shaping the nature of his lordship. Instead, as Wainwright argued, the Verturian victory at Dunnichen, in addition to being symptomatic of the changing face of the relationship between Mercia and Northumbria, 'reflects rather than changes the true political balance in the north'.[37] We have seen that the star of the kingdom of Fortriu appears to have been on the rise in the years leading up to Dunnichen, with Bridei extending his *imperium* into neighbouring Pictish regions while Ecgfrith strove to recover from defeat on the Trent. The events of 20 May 685 may be seen as symptomatic of these important adjustments of the political landscape in northern Britain, and it is in this regard in particular that we may speak of what Marren has called the 'far-reaching consequences' of the battle of Dunnichen. We may even follow his suggestion that Bridei's victory 'influenced profoundly the course of history in the north and east of Scotland',[38] although it is important not to over-dramatise here. It seems to the present writer that the outcome of the battle may be seen as having bought Bridei and his successors after 693 the breathing room to consolidate the gains that he had made in his aggressive campaigns of the latter half of his reign. The end result of this process was the successful and enduring establishment of Verturian hegemony over much of lowland Pictavia, bringing with it the added bonus that any subsequent Northumbrian attempt to dominate the king of Fortriu will have found that the task had become significantly more formidable than had ever been the case before.

For the most part the precise political and other details

involved here are frustratingly obscure, though there is evidence that important changes were introduced to political terminology north of the Forth during the reign of Bridei as king of Fortriu. For example, Northumbrian notions that southern Pictavia was made up of 'innumerable nations' and 'kingdoms' at the outset of Bridei's kingship – of which Fortriu was undoubtedly one – seem to give way by the end of Bede's life to the idea that all Pictish territory south of the Grampians constituted a single kingdom to which the name Fortriu was applied by Gaelic observers. The process whereby these other Pictish kingdoms became suppressed as *regiones* within an aggressively expansionist Verturian kingdom appears to have begun with Bridei's campaigns of the early 680s. It is therefore reasonable to suspect that his victory over Ecgfrith in 685, enabling him to keep for himself the resources that he had formerly been required to send to his over-king in tribute, was an important step in the formation and consolidation of this new Verturian hegemony. In another study the present writer has considered evidence relating to parallel ecclesiastical developments that appear to have been obtained in Fortriu as a result of such political change. These seem to have included the establishment of a single Church overseen by a bishop based at Abernethy, the diversion of considerable resources on the part of Verturian potentates into the foundation and enrichment of churches (employed among other things for the provision of the distinctive Pictish ecclesiastical sculpture of which there are many surviving examples), and the establishment of the Columban *familia* as the dominant force in the Verturian Church for a generation after the death of Bridei.[39] One cannot say with any certainty, given the nature of the evidence, that such political and ecclesiastical developments would never have occurred had Bridei not won the battle of Dunnichen. It is even less apparent that Fortriu cannot have emerged as the most substantial kingdom in northern Britain – and the one from which the kingdom of Scots was ultimately to grow – had things not gone Bridei's way on that fateful May afternoon. These are things that we cannot know, but on balance there are grounds for suspicion that Fortriu would have developed with a different face and a different form had Ecgfrith been victorious, had he managed to topple Bridei from his kingship and had he succeeded in preserving the tributary status of the Verturian kingdom for another generation.

One particular ecclesiastical development is worthy of special comment here in closing. It is interesting that the new stone church famously commissioned some thirty years after the battle by the Verturian king, Naiton son of Derilei, built for him by Anglian stonemasons sent from Bede's monastery of Wearmouth-Jarrow and dedicated to Wearmouth's patron saint, is thought to have stood on the site now occupied by Restenneth Priory church.[40] This identification, like so much that we have seen throughout the present work, is far from certain. It is nevertheless fascinating to consider the symbolism that would have accompanied the erection of a church on this promontory that once overlooked Restenneth Loch – our *Linn Garan* or *Nechtanesmere*. It was constructed with Anglian assistance and expertise, much as the kingdom over which Naiton held sway may be thought to have owed much in its form and institutions to examples set for Bridei and his successors by Oswig and Ecgfrith. It was commissioned by a successor of the victor of Dunnichen but built by masons sent by a Northumbrian monastery endowed by Ecgfrith and the scene of one of the last (perhaps the very last) ecclesiastical functions he ever attended, allowing Naiton's church to symbolise the extent to which the era of *gueith* between Bridei, his *fratruelis* and their two peoples had receded into the past. Finally, from the grounds of this new church building dedicated to St Peter, under whose protection Naiton had recently placed his 'reformed nation', one might gaze eastwards across the battlefield and infamous *linn* or *mere* where the future viability of the Verturian hegemony had been so emphatically demonstrated to Pict and Angle alike and affirmed by divine providence. If we accept the identification of Restenneth with Naiton's church, then, it is possible to detect within its construction and siting a subtle blending of the past, present and future of the kingdom of Fortriu and the significance of the Dunnichen battlefield in all three respects. Within such a scenario it is difficult to think of a more likely original setting for the cross-slab that stands now a few miles further along the B9134 in the yard of Aberlemno kirk – formerly a dependency of Restenneth Priory – and commemorates so exquisitely on one side the important battle fought on the shores of Restenneth Loch on 20 May 685.[41]

Conclusion: Looking Ahead at Looking Back at Dunnichen

Modern historians can be notorious kill-joys. In the specific context of Scottish history, one need look back no further than the forlorn hanging and shaking of some academic heads as Hollywood's fanciful interpretation of what was already a fanciful version of the story of William Wallace highlighted once more the gulf that often separates what 'sells' from what meets the rigorous requirements of modern historical inquiry. Similarly, most prior examinations of the battle of Dunnichen have tended to portray its background and significance in much more evocative and dramatic terms than have been favoured here. If the battle has any modern-day relevance for readers in Scotland or anywhere else as 'the birthplace of the Scottish nation' the present writer has not attempted to frame it, and this study has been consistently critical throughout – and perhaps overly so – of other, more romanticised, versions of the story that are on offer. Such works are not without their merits for not sharing the remit which the present writer has set for himself. Those interested not just in the battle of Dunnichen itself, but also in the manner in which it has been interpreted and appreciated by generations of scholars in Scotland and elsewhere, are encouraged to read further afield and to sample for themselves the variety of literature that exists on the subject. Only in that way can readers hope to decide for themselves whether or not modern Scotland was born on 20 May 685.

In endeavouring to place Ecgfrith's campaign and Bridei's victory more firmly into their contemporary historical context than has hitherto been attempted, the present work has arrived at a number of new conclusions about the circumstances surrounding the battle of Dunnichen and the general course of the fighting itself. Its departure from other studies in these regards has not, however, been complete. Despite having tended throughout to follow its own markedly different path through the evidence, in the very final analysis nothing has been presented here to contradict either Peter Marren's belief that Dunnichen was 'the scene of the most resounding victory the Picts ever won' or even Graeme Cruickshank's more grandiose conception of the battle as ranking 'among the great and decisive battles of Scotland'. The present writer is motivated to support both characterisations. As a Scottish – or at least northern British – historical event of considerable note, the battle of Dunnichen is probably no less worthy of popular attention and acclaim than such better known engagements as Culloden and Bannockburn, even if it is never likely to rival either in any significant way. Though we have here taken issue with the suggestion that 'it is no exaggeration to say that it [the battle] created the circumstances which allowed the embryo Scottish nation to materialise and to grow to maturity',[2] it is only fair to emphasise that the more romanticised interpretations of these other, more famous, evocative Scottish battles have come under similar fire in academic circles in recent times.

Designs upon the fabric of Dunnichen Hill itself on the part of the quarrying industry as recently as 1991 have highlighted the site's profound lack of status as compared to these other mainstays of the Scottish tourist industry. There is at present a gravel pit situated probably within the bounds of the early historic loch and a golf course which may lie on ground upon which the battle of Dunnichen was fought. Quarrying and golf must, of course, be conducted somewhere – both the *Statistical Account of Scotland* (1791–1799) and the *New Statistical Account* (1845) describe how important the quarrying industry has been for centuries for the area's economy – and the present work is not intended to enter into any debates on either side.[3] It may be pointed out that it is difficult to imagine either the Bannockburn or the Culloden battlefield sites coming under such serious threat, but such a degree of protection has been available to few Scottish battlefield sites, some of which – the example of Stirling Bridge leaps to mind – seem hardly less historically significant than Dunnichen. How much protection is due such a site, and if protection were on offer, what exactly might reasonably be protected? The higher profile that would inevitably attend large-scale protection of Dunnichen Hill and its environs would attract a range of enthusiasts of various strands (particularly on and around 20 May), bringing with them a range of potential effects, positive and negative, upon the locality, its economy and its individual inhabitants, businesses and property owners. These are issues for local and national governments to sort out in their own best interests. Perhaps above all else the recent history of Dunnichen Hill as a site of historical and industrial interest has emphasised the need to ensure that, if the site is not to be protected in whole or in part, at least it is made clear what stands to be lost if quarrying, impromptu pilgrimages, and other activities are allowed to go ahead. Only time will tell if the present work, considered alongside the rest of the historiography on the subject of Dunnichen, will have anything at all to contribute in this regard.

With regard to the battle of Dunnichen itself, it would be heartening to think that there remains evidence of an archaeological nature yet to be discovered that will one day help us to better understand and more precisely and definitively locate the engagement. Wainwright, an accomplished archaeologist himself, was not optimistic on this score:

> Battle-sites, unlike fortresses and dwellings, are notoriously elusive; they seldom leave clear traces of themselves for the archaeologist, and it is doubtful if the use of modified mine-detectors in the future will do much to reveal the many unknown sites of battles. Neither victors nor vanquished would normally leave valuable weapons and other loot lying on the field of battle, and what remained would be thoroughly gleaned by the local population...
> It would probably be a waste of time to seek a battle-site as the term is generally understood. The most one would expect to find would be a mass of human remains buried

without much ceremony… [and] in any case the swamp
probably claimed many bodies – dead as well as alive.[4]

Wainwright voiced this view in an article in which he
presented the results of a painstaking survey of the former
extent of Dunnichen Moss; on the present model a similar
survey of the extent of the early historic loch we have
called Restenneth Loch and identified as the 'crane lake'
would be most welcome. The possibility, remote as it may
be, that the anaerobic environment at the bottom of this
loch preserved relics of the battle subsequently buried
in sediment might perhaps be explored. Modern (and
future) surveying techniques and technology quite beyond
Wainwright's reckoning in 1948, including geophysical
survey, might leave marginally more room for optimism
with regard to future discoveries than he thought.

Quite apart from the battlefield itself, there is much
archaeological work to be done in its environs and in Angus
generally that can only increase our ability to contextualise
the battle. The subject of Pictish route-ways has already
been mentioned with regard to Ecgfrith's approach to the
field of battle, and it would also be interesting to know how
his Verturian opponents got there. Investigations into the
size of the population of the land visible from the summit
of Turin Hill would help to give us some indication of the
number of men that were available to be called into service
by Bridei. Excavation work at Dún Nechtain (once satis-
factorily located!), Kemp's Castle on Turin Hill, and sites of
lesser status in the region would flesh out our understanding of the objects of Ecgfrith's campaigning. Since the late
eighteenth century it has been believed that the remains

of the eponymous stronghold lay upon 'a low shoulder' projecting from the south side of Dunnichen Hill, though 'the stones of the fort or castle… have been removed to build fences; and its area has been nearly obliterated by a quarry'.[5] It is possible, however, that our commentators misidentified these stony remains and that there is work to be done at Dún Nechtain: Wainwright, for his part, believed that 'a few stones and the broken line of what seems to have been a stone wall or earthwork' still to be found below the south side of the summit were worthy of investigation as the remains of the stronghold.[6] In recent times, of course, a mast has been erected on the summit of Dunnichen Hill – has this obliterated the last shreds of evidence that might have been recovered from the site? Finally, the potentially important site of Restenneth Priory has never been dug in the interests of settling debates of long standing about the antiquity of its upstanding remains and the history of occupation there.

We began this study with Mr Cruickshank's view of the battle of Dunnichen as having been 'one of the biggest clashes of arms in the history of "Dark Age" Britain'. Unfortunately, it is simply impossible to know this, and inadvisable to even assume it. One's sense of how 'big' the battle was in real terms ought not to be influenced by one's views about how 'big' it was in terms of its significance, and there is nothing in the surviving record to indicate that the size or scale of the battle of Dunnichen was anything other than of a kind with the rather lengthy roll of other contemporary battles. One must take similar care in speaking of Dunnichen as 'one of the most crucial battles in the "Dark Age" history of Britain', much less as 'one of the most important events in the history of the north'.[7] We have seen that the battle was almost certainly both crucial and important from many different contemporary perspectives – and particularly from Bridei's own – yet such opinions of its significance strike the present writer as excessively grandiose. This study is perhaps unlikely to dissuade from a view of this kind most readers who hold one, and even among those who may find much else in the preceding chapters that satisfies them, there will no doubt be those who would disagree with the author on this last point. As a final thought on this matter, then, it will be said only that readers are, of course, entitled to their opinions, contrary or otherwise, on this or any other point that has been raised here, no matter how shaky the ground upon which such views stand appears to this author, and no matter how much they may appear to him to be based ultimately upon faith rather than fact. One can hardly be dogmatic about one's interpretations of such an incomplete body of evidence, and the requirements of the historian's profession represent only some of those which might be brought to bear upon the subject.

Appendix 1

The Anonymous
Vita Sancti Cudberti

The anonymous *Life of Saint Cuthbert* was written at Lindisfarne in the last years of the reign of Ecgfrith's successor Aldfrith. The purpose of this work was to extol the virtuous life of Cuthbert, whom Ecgfrith had appointed to the see of Hexham shortly before his death, after which the bishop switched sees in order to acquire the see of Lindisfarne. Among its many stories intent upon showing the ways in which Cuthbert's sanctity was made manifest during his lifetime are episodes in which it is claimed that the bishop received prophetic foreknowledge about the fate of Ecgfrith at Dunnichen. Fortunately, a number of incidental details are provided that give important information about the battle, and some of these are fleshed out still further in Bede's expanded version of this same text written some twenty years later. The author, whoever he was, is likely to have been at the height of his monastic career at the time of the battle of Dunnichen. He makes several poignant references to the sense of shock, the sadness and the bitterness that he and his contemporaries experienced when they heard word of the death of their king. It seems not to have been until the subsequent generation that men like Stephan and Bede began to form hypotheses to explain why God had willed Ecgfrith's destruction.

On the Death and Successor of Ecgfrith

iii.6.   *De finiendo uite Ecfridi regis prophetia eius et herede et episco-patu eius.*

Preterea sanctimonialis uirgo et regalis Aelfleda abbatissa sanctum ana-choritam Dei humiliter in nomine Domini in obuiam sibi nauigare ad Cocuaedesae petiuit. Cui ancilla Dei flectens genua, multa interrogare cepit. Postremo autem per nomen Domini nostri Iesu Christi et per nouem ordines angelorum, et omnium sanctorum personas, fiducialiter adiurauit, interrogans de longitudine uitae fratris sui regis Egfridi. Ipse autem homo Dei grauiter adiuratus, timens Dominum, cepit dicere de breuitate uite hominis circuitu uerborum, et adiunxit dicens, O ancilla Dei, numquid non paruum est licet aliquis uiuat xii menses? Illa uero statim arripiens mente de rege esse dictum, amaro fletu lacrimauit. Sicut ei et multis aliis post anni spatium casus regalium a maligna manu hostilis gladii omnem amaritudinem renouauit. Adhuc adiunxit dicens, Per eandem unitatem et trinitatem supradictam adiuro te ut dicas quem heredem habebit. Ipse etiam paululum tacens dixit, Illum autem non minus tibi esse fratrem usurpaueris, quam alterum. Hoc quippe et incredibile uidebatur, diligentius tamen inter-rogauit, in quo loco esset. Ipse uero patienter sustinens eam ait, O serua Dei, quid miraris licet sit in aliqua insula super hoc mare? Illa iam cito rememorauit de Aldfrido qui nunc regnat pacifice fuisse dictum, qui tunc erat in insula quam Ii nominant...

iii.6. How he prophesied the end of the life of King Ecgfrith, and about his heir, and about his episcopate.

There was, furthermore, a certain sanctimonious virgin and royal abbess Aelfleda, who humbly asked the holy hermit of God in the name of the Lord to cross the sea and meet her at [Coquet Island]. On bended knees, this handmaiden of God began asking many questions. Finally she adjured him boldly, in the name of our Lord Jesus Christ, the nine orders of angels and the persons of all the saints, asking about the length of the life of King Ecgfrith her brother. Now therefore the man of God, having been so solemnly

adjured and fearing the Lord, began to speak with evasive words
about the brevity of the life of men, and he added these words: 'O
handmaiden of God, is it not but a short time if a man were to live
twelve months?' At once realising that he spoke of the king, she
wept bitter tears. And the fall of the members of the royal house by
the cruel hand of a hostile sword after the space of a year renewed
all the bitterness for her and for many others. Then she added these
words: 'By the same unity and trinity aforementioned I adjure you
to say whom he will have as an heir.' For a short time he was silent,
then said, 'You will accept him to be no less a brother to you than
the other.' This indeed seemed so incredible that she asked him dili-
gently in what place he was. And verily he said, patiently forbearing
her, 'O handmaiden of God, why should you wonder though he
is on some island beyond this sea?' Then she quickly remembered
that he spoke of Aldfrith who now reigns in peace, who was then
on the island that they call [Iona]…

On the Outcome of the Battle of Dunnichen

iv.8. *De die et tempore horaque occisionis Ecgfridi regis.*

*Eo tempore quo Ecgfridus rex Pictorum regionem depopulans, postremo
tamen secundum praedestinatum iudicium Dei superandus et occidendus
uastabat, sanctus episcopus noster ad ciuitatem Luel pergens, uisitauit reginam illic rei effectum exspectantem. Sabbato ergo die, sicut presbiteri et
diaconi ex quibus multi adhuc supersunt adfirmauerunt, hora nona consid-
erantibus illis murum ciuitatis, et fontem in ea a Romanis mire olim con-
structum, secundum id quod Uacha ciuitatis praepositus ducens eos reuelauit.
Stans episcopus iuxta baculum sustentationis, inclinato capite ad terram
deorsum, et iterum eleuatis oculis ad celum suspirans ait, O O O, existimo
enim perpetratum esse bellum, iudicatumque est iudicium de populis nostris
bellantibus aduersum. Tunc iam diligenter sciscitantibus illis quid factum
esset, scire uolentibus occultans respondit, O filioli mei considerate, quam
admirabilis sit aer, et recolite quam inscrutabilia sunt iudicia Dei, et reliqua.
Itaque post paucos dies miserabile et lacrimabile bellum in eadem hora et
eadem die qua ille ostensum est longe lateque nuntiatum esse audierunt.*

iv.8. Of the day and hour of the slaying of King Ecgfrith.

At the time when King Ecgfrith was ravaging and laying waste to the *regio* of the Picts – though finally he was to be overcome and slain according to the predestined judgement of God – our holy bishop went to the *ciuitas* of [Carlisle] to visit the queen who was awaiting the issue of events there. On Saturday, as the priests and deacons declare (of whom many still survive), at the ninth hour they were looking at the town wall and the well formerly built in a wonderful manner by the Romans (as Wacha, the *praepositus* of the town who was conducting them, explained). The bishop meanwhile stood leaning upon his staff, head inclined towards the ground, and then he lifted his eyes heavenwards and said with a sigh, 'O O O! I think that a battle is over and that judgement has been given against our people in the war.' Then, when they urgently asked him what had happened and desired to know, he evasively said, 'O my sons, look at the sky – consider how wonderful it is and think how inscrutable are the judgements of God' and so on. And so, after a few days, they learned that it had been announced far and wide that a wretched and mournful battle had taken place at the very day and hour in which it had been revealed to him.

Appendix 2

Stephan's *Vita Sancti Wilfrithi*

Stephan was a priest and probably a monk like Bede. He has been traditionally identified with a contemporary choir-master called Eddius Stephanus – his *Life of Saint Wilfrith* has been published several times under this name – but scholars now doubt the validity of this identification and refer to him simply as Stephan. He seems to have been attached to or a member of the community of the monastery of Ripon. It was at this monastery in the early 660s that Wilfrith, later Bishop of York and still later Bishop of Hexham, began his remarkable ecclesiastical career by becoming abbot, and it seems always to have held a special place in his heart. Wilfrith was a complicated and controversial man both in life and after his death, and Stephan's *Life* is a work of unabashed apology on his behalf. Here Wilfrith is portrayed as having been a pivotal historical figure who was at the centre of the important ecclesiastical developments that took place during his career; Bede, who used the text as a source, went some of the way in accepting this point of view, but also muddied the water by arguing that certain other individuals were primarily responsible for much that Stephan ascribes to Wilfrith alone. Stephan wrote this work in the years around 720, and he had access to a considerable archive of Wilfrith's correspondence and other documents no doubt provided to him by Acca, Wilfrith's hand-picked successor in the see of Hexham, who sponsored Stephan in his writing and was also an occasional patron of Bede, who lived and worked in his diocese. Bede's reputation has tended to mean that scholars consistently trust his word over Stephan's where they differ on points of historical fact or interpretation, but Stephan's version of events ought not to be so readily dismissed. That being said, the apologetic aspect of Stephan's *Life* must always be kept in mind, and it is important not to fall into the trap of confusing hagiography with biography.

On the Battle of the Two Rivers

§ 19. *De uictoria regis in feroces Pictos.*

In diebus autem illis Ecfrithus rex religiosus cum beatissima regina Aethiltrythae, cuius corpus vivens ante impollutum post mortem incorruptum manens adhuc demonstrat, simul in unum Wilfritho episcopo in omnibus oboedientes facti, pax et gaudium in populis et anni frugiferi victoriaeque in hostes, Deo adiuvante, subsecutae sunt. Sicut enim iuvenis Ioas rex Iuda, Ioada sacerdote magno vivente adhuc, Deo placuit et in hostes triumphavit: mortuo vero sacerdote, Deo displicuit et regnum minuit, ita, Ecfritho rege in concordia pontificis nostri vivente, secundum multorum testimonium regnum undique per victorias triumphales augebatur: concordia vero inter eos sopita et regina supradicta ab eo separata et Deo dicata, triumphus in diebus regis desinit. Nam in primis annis eius tenero adhuc regno populi bestiales Pictorum feroci animo subiectionem Saxonum despiciebant et iugum servitutis proicere a se minabant; congregantes undique de utribus et folliculis aquilonis innumeras gentes, quasi formicarum greges in aestate de tumulis verrentes aggerem contra domum cadentem muniebant. Nam, quo audito, rex Ecgfrithus, humilis in populis suis, magnanimus in hostes, statim equitatui exercitu praeparato, tarda molimina nesciens, sicut Iudas Machabeus in Deum confidens, parva manu populi Dei contra inormem et supra invisibilem hostem cum Beornheth audaci subregulo invasit strategemque immensam populi subruit, duo flumina cadaveribus mortuorum replentes, ita, quod mirum dictu est, ut supra siccis pedibus ambulantes, fugientium turbam occidentes persequebantur: et in servitutem redacti, populi usque ad diem occisionis regis captivitatis iugo subiecti iacebant.

§ 19. Of the king's victory over the ferocious Picts.

Now in those days a pious King Ecgfrith, with the most blessed Queen Aeðilthryð (whose body, remaining still uncorrupted after death, shows that it was unstained beforehand while alive), were both obedient to Bishop Wilfrith in all things; there ensued, by the aid of God, peace and joy among the people, fruitful years, and victory over their foes. For, as when Joash, king of Judah, was young, so long as Jehoiada the great high priest was alive he pleased God and triumphed over his enemies – but when the priest was dead he displeased God and diminished his kingdom; so, when King Ecgfrith lived at peace with our bishop, the kingdom (as many bear witness) was increased on every hand by his glorious victories – but when the concord between them was destroyed and his queen had separated from him and dedicated herself to God, the king's triumph came to an end during his own lifetime. Yet in his first years, while the kingdom was still weak, the bestial Pictish peoples had a fierce contempt for subjection to the Saxon and threatened to throw off from themselves the yoke of servitude. They gathered together innumerable nations from every nook and corner of the north, like a swarm of ants in the summer, sweeping from their hills, heap up a mound to protect their tottering house. So King Ecgfrith, when he heard, lowly as he was among his own folk and magnanimous towards his foes, forthwith assembled a mounted force, being a stranger to tardy operations, and trusting in God (like Judas Maccabaeus) and assisted by the brave *subregulus* Beornheth he attacked with his little band of God's people an enemy host that was vast and, moreover, concealed. He slew an enormous number of the people, filling two rivers with corpses so that – wondrous to relate – the slayers, passing dry-foot over the rivers, pursued and slew a crowd of fugitives. The peoples were reduced to servitude and remained subject under the yoke of captivity until the time when the king was killed.

On the Battle of Dunnichen

§ 44. Quomodo Aldfrithus rex suscepit pontificem nostrum.

Factum est itaque, postquam vergentibus annorum multorum circulis, sancto rectore nostro aliquando honorifice in exilio degente, et tunc monachis suis per diversa loca totius Brittanniae exterminatis et sub alienis dominis moerentes expectantesque a Domino redemptionem, ut postremo audierunt miserrimae cladis ruinam, Ecgfritho Ultrahumbrensium rege occiso et cum omni optimo exercitus sui agmine a gente Pictorum oppresso. Et post eum Aldfrithus rex sapientissimus regnavit, qui sanctum Wilfrithum episcopum nostrum de exilio secundo anno regni sui venerabiliter secundum praeceptum archiepiscopi ad se invitavit…

§ 44. How King Aldfrith received our bishop.

And so it happened that there followed the passing away of a circle of many years – our holy prelate was at the time living honourably in exile, and his monks had been banished and scattered into diverse places throughout the whole of Britain and were mourning under the power of foreign lords, awaiting redemption from the Lord. So at last they heard about a most woeful disaster – Ecgfrith, king of the Northumbrians, had been slain and overcome by the nation of the Picts with all the flower of his army. And after him reigned the most wise King Aldfrith, who in the second year of his reign, in accordance with the archbishop's command, summoned to him our holy bishop Wilfrith from exile…

Appendix 3

Bede's *Historia Ecclesiastica Gentis Anglorum*

Bede, whose name was actually Beda, was twelve years old and living in the monastery of Jarrow as a novice when Ecgfrith attended the dedication of its church to St Paul only a month before the battle of Dunnichen. Though his account of the death of Ecgfrith in his *Ecclesiastical History of the Anglian Nation* was not written, as he tells us, for another forty-six years, the shock and despair of his elders seems to have made a lasting impression upon the boy who would grow to become Anglo-Saxon England's most respected and venerated man of letters. Bede was first and foremost a wise and respected biblical scholar, but he was also fascinated by time and chronology and, as he grew older, he became interested in where his Christianity had come from – how the religion had come to and developed among his people. In addition to his many works of biblical scholarship, Bede spent a lifetime re-calibrating historical dates according to his favoured chronological system, thus becoming one of the earliest Western thinkers to think in terms of *anni domini*, counting the 'years of the Lord' from the Nativity – still the basis of the 'AD' dating convention used today. As a historian, Bede was neither the unimpeachable authority nor the dull-witted purveyor of worthless gossip that has sometimes been envisioned by his admirers and detractors – he was a careful and thorough scholar who made use of a range of written and anecdotal evidence, but he also seems to have placed his trust in some unreliable sources from time to time, and his interpretations of past events were coloured by his different motives in telling the story of his people's Christian past. As a result, though Bede is generally trustworthy, he must be read with care, and wherever possible his information should be compared with that provided by other sources. With regard to his account of the battle of Dunnichen, Bede seems to have pieced together different sources of reliable information, and one may detect both a Gaelic and an Anglian viewpoint in different parts of the narrative.

On Berct's Expedition and the Battle of Dunnichen

iv.26. *Anno dominicae incarnationis DCLXXXIIII Ecgfrid rex Nordanhymbrorum, misso Hiberniam cum exercitu duce Bercto, uastauit misere gentem innoxiam et nationi Anglorum semper amicissimam, ita ut ne ecclesiis quidem aut monasteriis manus parceret hostilis. At insulani et, quantum ualuere, armis arma repellebant, et inuocantes diuinae auxilium pietatis caelitus se uindicari continuis diu inprecationibus postulabant. Et quamuis maledici regnum Dei possidere non possint, creditum est tamen quod hi qui merito inpietatis suae maledicebantur, ocius Domino uindice poenas sui reatus luerent. Siquidem anno post hunc proximo idem rex, cum temere exercitum ad uastandam Pictorum prouinciam duxisset, multum prohibentibus amicis et maxime beatae memoriae Cudbercto, qui nuper fuerat ordinatus episcopus, introductus est simulantibus fugam hostibus in angustias inaccessorum montium, et cum maxima parte copiarum, quas secum adduxerat, extinctus anno aetatis suae XLmo, regni autem XVmo, die tertio decimo kalendarum Iuniarum. Et quidem, ut dixi, prohibuerunt amici, ne hoc bellum iniret; sed quoniam anno praecedente noluerat audire reuerentissimum patrem Ecgberctum, ne Scottiam nil se laedentem inpugnaret, datum est illi ex poena peccati illius, ne nunc eos, qui ipsum ab interitu reuocare cupiebant, audiret. Ex quo tempore spes coepit et uirtus regni Anglorum 'fluere ac retro sublapsa referri'. Nam et Picti terram possessionis suae quam tenuerunt Angli, et Scotti qui erant in Brittania, Brettonum quoque pars nonnulla libertatem receperunt; quam et hactenus habent per annos circiter XLVI. Vbi inter plurimos gentis Anglorum uel interemtos gladio uel seruitio addictos uel de terra Pictorum fuga lapsos, etiam reuerentissimus uir Domini Trumuini, qui in eos episcopatum acceperat, recessit cum suis, qui erant in monasterio Aebbercurnig, posito quidem in regione Anglorum sed in uicinia freti, quod Anglorum terras Pictorumque disterminat.*

iv.26. In the year of our Lord 684 Ecgfrith, king of the Northumbrians, sent the *dux* Berct to Ireland with an army, which wretchedly wasted a people that was harmless and that had always been most friendly to the Anglian nation, and the hostile bands spared neither churches nor monasteries. And the islanders, insofar as they were able, resisted force with force, while imploring merciful divine assistance and invoking the vengeance of God with unceasing imprecations. And although those who curse cannot inherit the kingdom of God, yet one may believe that those who were justly cursed for their wickedness quickly suffered the penalty of their guilt at the vengeful hand of the Lord. Indeed in the very next year the same king rashly led an army to waste the kingdom of the Picts against the urgent advice of friends – and mostly Cuthbert of blessed memory, who had recently been consecrated a bishop. He was led by an enemy feigning flight into a tight place of inaccessible mountains, and there he was killed with the greater part of the forces he had taken with him on [20 May] in the fortieth year of his age and the fifteenth of his reign. And as I have said, his friends urged him not to undertake this war; but in the previous year he had refused to listen to the most reverend father Ecgberct, who had urged him not to attack the Irish who had done him no harm – and the punishment for his sin was that he would not now listen to those who sought to save him from his own destruction. From this time the hopes and strength of the Anglian kingdom began to ebb and fall away. For the Picts recovered their own land which the Angles had formerly held, and the Irish who were in Britain and some part of the Britons recovered their liberty; which they have now enjoyed for about forty-six years. Many of the Anglian nation were either slain by the sword or taken captive or escaped by flight from the land of the Picts, including the most reverend man of God Trumwini, who had accepted their episcopate; he retired with his community who were in the monastery of Abercorn, which was in an Anglian *regio* but close to the firth which divides the territories of the Angles and the Picts.

Appendix 4

Historia Brittonum

There are several different versions (or recensions) of *Historia Brittonum* ('History of the Britons' or 'British History'), each of which is unique. They all seem to be based upon a common original text composed in North Wales from a range of different sources in the middle third of the ninth century, about 150 years after the battle of Dunnichen. The text is problematic and contains much that is fantastic, and is probably best known for what it purports about Arthur (§56). Its information about Dunnichen is couched within a genealogical tract about the Bernician royal house which shows little sign of being much older than the time of Bede. We have little reason to mistrust its evidence. There is some key information here that is preserved nowhere else, including the fact that Ecgfrith and Bridei were *fratrueles* and a British name for the battle which I take as being its Pictish one: *Gueith Linn Garan*.

On Ecgfrith

§57. *Woden genuit Beldeg* [etc. down to Ida]. *Ida autem duodecim filios habuit, quorum nomina sunt: Adda, Aedldric, Decdric, Edric, Deothere, Osmer, et unam reginam Bearnoch, Ealric. Ealdric genuit Aelfret. Ipse est Aedlferd Flesaur. Nam et ipse habuit filios septem, quorum nomina sunt: Anfrid, Osguald, Osbiu, Osguid, Osgudu, Oslapf, Offa. Osguid genuit Alcfrid, et Aelfguin, et Echfrid. Echgfrid ipse est qui fecit bellum contra fratruelem suum, qui erat rex Pictorum, nomine Birdei, et ibi corruit cum omni robore exercitus sui, et Picti cum rege suo victores extiterunt, et numquam addiderunt Saxones ambronum ut a Pictis vectigal exigerent. A tempore istius belli vocatur Gueith Lin Garan. Osguid autem habuit duas uxores, quarum una vocabatur Rieinmelth, filia Royth, filii Rum, et altera vocabatur Eanfled, filia Eadguin, filii Alli.*

§57. Woden begot Beldeg [etc. down to Ida]. And Ida had twelve sons, who were named Adda, Aedldric, Decdric, Edric, Deothere, Osmer, and one Queen Bearnoch, Ealric. Ealdric begot [Aeðilfrith]. He is [Aeðilfrith] Twister. And he had seven sons, who were named [Eanfrith], [Oswald], Osbiu, [Oswig], Osgudu, Oslapf, Offa. [Oswig] begot [Alchfrith], and [Aelfwini], and [Ecgfrith]. [Ecgfrith] is the one who made war against his *fratruelis*, who was the Pictish king called [Bridei], and he fell there with all the strength of his army, and the Picts with their king emerged as victors, and the Saxon thugs never grew thence to exact tribute from the Picts. From that time the battle is called *Gueith Lin Garan* ['battle of crane lake']. And [Oswig] had two wives, of whom one was called Rieinmelth daughter of Royth son of [Run], and the other was called Eanfled daughter of [Eadwini] son of [Alle].

Appendix 5

The 'Chronicle of Ireland'

A careful analysis and comparison of the various surviving sets of Irish annals – year-by-year historical records – has shown that a text that scholars call the 'Chronicle of Ireland' was composed in Armagh in the first decade of the tenth century. It has also been shown that the tenth-century scholars who produced this text made use of several earlier chronicles, including one that had been kept more-or-less current at the monastery of Iona from the middle of the seventh century until the middle of the eighth. It appears to have been in this 'Iona Chronicle' that the battle of Dunnichen was recorded in the first instance, and in this way did it find its way first into the 'Chronicle of Ireland' some two centuries later, and thence into the different annal records based upon it that survive from the later Middle Ages.

On the Battle of the Two Rivers

AU 672.6 *Expulsio Drosto de regno…*
          Expulsion of Drust from the kingship…
AT   *Expuilsio Drosto de reghno…*
          Expulsion of Drust from the kingship…
AClon   Dregtus was expelled out of the kingdom…

On the Battle of the Trent

AU 680.4 *Bellum Saxonum ubi cecidit Ailmine filius Ossu.*
          A battle of the Saxons where [Aelfwini son of Oswig]
          fell.
AT   *Bellum Saxonum ubi cecidit Almuine filius Osu.*
          A battle of Saxons where [Aelfwini son of Oswig]
          fell.
AClon   The battle of the Saxons was given, where Almon son
          of K. Ossve was slaine.

On Bridei's Wars

AU 681.5 *Obsessio Duin Foither.*
          Siege of Dún Foither [Dunnottar].
AU 682.4 *Orcades deletae sunt la Bruide.*
          The *Orcades* [Orkney] were annihilated by Bridei.
AT   *Orcades deletae sunt la Bruidhe.*
          The *Orcades* [Orkney] were annihilated by Bridei.
AU 683.3 *Obsesio Duin Att & obsessio Dúin Duirn.*
          Siege of Dún At [Dunadd] and siege of Dún Duirn
          [Dundurn].

On Berct's Expedition

AU 685.2 *Saxones Campum Bregh uastant & aeclesias plurimas in mense Iuni.*
    Saxons waste Mag Breg and many churches in the month of June.

AT   *Saxones Campum uastauerunt, et eclesias plurimas, in mense Iuni.*
    Saxons wasted the plain, and many churches, in the month of June.

AClon   The Saxons, the plains of Moyebrey with Divers churches wasted and destroyed in the month of June, for the alliance of the Irish with the Brittaines.

It is by comparing the Annals of Ulster with one of the annals of the so-called 'Clonmacnoise group' (Annals of Tigernach, Annals of Clonmacnoise) that scholars can reconstruct the contents of the 'Chronicle of Ireland'. The phrase 'for the alliance of the Irish with the Brittaines' does not appear in AU or AT, and it may or may not have been present in the 'Chronicle of Ireland'.

On the Battle of Dunnichen

AU 686.1 *Bellum Duin Nechtain uicisimo die mensis Maii, Sabbati die, factum est, in quo Etfrith m. Ossu, rex Saxonum, .x.u. anno regni sui consummata magna cum caterua militum suorum interfectus est.*
    The battle of Dún Nechtain fought on the twentieth day of the month of May, a Saturday, in which [Ecgfrith son of Oswig], king of Saxons, having completed the fifteenth year of his reign, was killed with the greater part of his warriors.

AT   *Cath Duin Nechtain uicesimo die mensis Maii, sabbati die factum est, in quo Ecfrith mac Osu, rex Saxonum, quinto decimo anno reighni sui consummato, magna cum caterua militum suorum interfectus est la Bruidhi mac Bili regis Fortrenn.*

The battle of Dún Nechtain fought on the twentieth day of the month of May, a Saturday, in which [Ecgfrith son of Oswig], king of Saxons, having completed the fifteenth year of his reign, was killed with the greater part of his warriors by [Bridei map Beli], king of Fortriu.

The phrase *la Bruidhi mac Bili regis Fortrenn* ('by Bridei map Beli, king of Fortriu') appears in AT but not in AU, which means that we cannot be certain that it was present in the 'Chronicle of Ireland' (nor that it was not).

Appendix 6

Iniu feras Bruide cath

The poem *Iniu feras Bruide cath* is preserved in a single manuscript – that of the so-called 'Fragmentary Annals of Ireland' – where it is attributed to one Riaguil of Bangor and is misplaced as if the 'son of Oswig' in question were Ecgfrith's successor Aldfrith. While it is not without its interpretative problems, not least with regard to its date, the poem provides an intriguing perspective upon the battle of Dunnichen and its importance outside of Fortriu.

1	*Iniu feras Bruide cath*	Today Bridei gives battle
2	*im forba a senathar,*	over the land of his grandfather,
3	*manad algas lá mac Dé*	unless it is the wish of the son of God
4	*conid é ad genathar.*	that restitution be made.
5	*Iniu ro bíth mac Ossa*	Today the son of Oswig was slain
6	*a ccath fria claidhmhe glasa;*	in battle against iron swords;
7	*cia do rada ait[h]irge,*	even though he did penance,
8	*is h-í ind-hí iar n-assa.*	it was penance too late.
9	*Iniu ro bíth mac Osa,*	Today the son of Oswig was slain,
10	*las(a) mbidis dubha deoga;*	who was wont to have dark drinks;
11	*ro cúala Críst ar nguidhe*	Christ has heard our prayer
12	*roisaorbut Bruide bregha.*	that Bridei would avenge Brega.

Line 8 is particularly problematic, since it can be and has been reconstructed in several different ways. Similarly the word *bregha* in line 12 has invited different translations down through the years; my own preference for 'Brega' simply does not work linguistically – a more exact translation would be 'Breo' – but I have taken it that there has been some mistake here and that the poem makes the same association between Berct's expedition and Ecgfrith's death that was made by Bede.

Appendix 7

Historia Dunelmensis Ecclesiae

The *History of the Church of Durham* is commonly attributed to Simeon of Durham, who flourished in the first quarter of the twelfth century. Although its testimony is late and essentially follows Bede for the period of interest to us, this text is important because it contains some additional information, including references to the place-name *Nechtanesmere* and to the burial of Ecgfrith on Iona.

On Ecgfrith

§9. ...*At rex Egfridus, anno quo fecerat hunc venerabilem patrem ordinari episcopum, cum maxima parte copiarum quas ad devastandam terram Pictorum secum duxerat, secundum prophetiam ejusdem patris Cuthberti extinctus est apud Nechtanesmere, quod est stagnum Nechtani, die xiii. kal. Juniarum, anno regni sui xv.; cujus corpus in Hii, insula Columbae, sepultum est.*

§9. ...But King Ecgfrith, in the year in which he had caused this venerable father to be consecrated a bishop, was slain with the greater part of the warriors he had brought with him to lay waste to the land of the Picts – as the same father Cuthbert had predicted – at *Nechtanesmere* (which is 'the lake of Nechtan'), on [20 May] in the fifteenth year of his reign. His body was buried on Iona, the island of Columba.

Notes

Chapter One

1 AU 686.1; the attribution of the victory to Bridei occurs in AT.

2 On the extent of Fortriu, see D. Broun, 'The Seven Kingdoms in *De situ Albanie*: A Record of Pictish political Geography or imaginary Map of ancient Alba?', in E.J. Cowan and R.A. McDonald (eds), *Alba: Celtic Scotland in the Middle Ages* (East Linton, 2000), 24–42, at 37–38.

3 The adjective 'Verturian' has been applied to those things pertaining to Fortriu by A. Woolf, 'The Verturian Hegemony: A Mirror in the North', in M.P. Brown and C.A. Farr (eds), *Mercia: An Anglo-Saxon Kingdom in Europe* (Leicester & New York, 2001), 106–11, at 107 and *passim*.

4 *HB* 57. On the Pictish language see in particular K. Forsyth, *Language in Pictland: the case against 'non-Indo-European Pictish'* (Utrecht, 1997); K.H. Jackson, 'The Pictish Language', in F.T. Wainwright (ed.), *The Problem of the Picts* (Edinburgh, 1955), 129–66.

5 *HDE* i.9. Scholars tend to follow Bede in referring to the Northumbrian peoples as Angles, but Oswig and Ecgfrith seem to have regarded themselves as Saxons.

6 G. Cruickshank, *The Battle of Dunnichen* (Balgavies, 1999), 6,
   20. There is an earlier edition of this work (Balgavies, 1991), of
   which the later version is almost entirely a recapitulation; all
   references will be to the 1999 edition unless otherwise noted.
7 G.D.R. Cruickshank, 'The Battle of Dunnichen and the
   Aberlemno Battle-Scene', in E.J. Cowan and R.A. McDonald
   (eds), *Alba: Celtic Scotland in the Middle Ages* (East Linton,
   2000), 69–87, at 72.
8 Cruickshank, *Dunnichen*, 6.
9 The most recent detailed examination of the sources
   is performed by L. Alcock, 'The Site of the "Battle of
   Dunnichen"', in *Scottish Historical Review* 75 (1996), 130–42, at
   131–36; see also F.T. Wainwright, 'Nechtanesmere', in *Antiquity*
   86 (1948), 82–97, at 82–86, Cruickshank, *Dunnichen*, 34–36.
10 This sculpture is of the type known as 'Class II' to specialists,
   indicating that it is an upright 'cross-slab' with a cross in
   relief on one side and some other scene (in this case a battle-
   scene) on the other. This system for the classification of the
   sculptured monuments of Scotland was devised by J. Romilly
   Allen and Joseph Anderson, and is outlined in their master
   work on the subject, *The Early Christian Monuments of Scotland*
   (Edinburgh, 1903), i, 3–4; now available in a new edition
   (Balgavies, 1993). The monument in question is described at ii,
   209–14, where it is classified as Aberlemno stone No. 2. A cast
   of the battle-scene is on display in the National Museum of
   Scotland, Edinburgh.
11 J. Romilly Allen, *ECMS*, ii, 211.
12 Cruickshank, 'Dunnichen and Aberlemno', 78. This essay
   contains Mr Cruickshank's most comprehensive discussion of
   the Aberlemno battle-scene to date (at 76–87), although 'a full-
   scale book, *The Aberlemno Battle-Scene*', is promised in the latest
   edition of his study on the battle (Cruickshank, *Dunnichen*, 7).
13 Recent affirmations of Cruickshank's view of the Aberlemno
   battle-scene as commemorative of Dunnichen include A.
   Ritchie, *Picts: an Introduction to the Life of the Picts and the
   Carved Stones in the Care of Historic Scotland* (Edinburgh, 1989),
   25–27; C. Cessford, 'Cavalry in Early Bernicia: a reply', in
   Northern History 79 (1993), 185–87, at 185; N. Hooper, 'The

Aberlemno Stone and Cavalry in Anglo-Saxon England', in
Northern History 79 (1993), 188–96, at 190; R. Oram, *Angus &
the Mearns: a Historical Guide* (Edinburgh, 1996), 88.

Chapter Two

1 Bede, *HE* iv.26.
2 Bede, *HE* ii.9–20. For a summary of the early evidence
   relating to the kingdoms of Bernicia and Deira, see B. Yorke,
   Kings and Kingdoms of Early Anglo-Saxon England (London &
   New York, 1990), 74–77.
3 Bede, *HE* ii.9.
4 Bede, *HE* i.22–ii.5.
5 Bede, *HE* iii.9. *Maserfelth*, or *bellum Cocboy* (ACamb 644),
   cannot be identified with absolute certainty, but is traditionally
   identified with Oswestry in Shropshire.
6 AU 639.3; 656.2.
7 Yorke, *Kings and Kingdoms*, 105.
8 AU 650.1. This clash between Oswig and Penda would seem
   to be alluded to by Bede, *HE* iii.16, where it is noted that,
   during the time of Áedán's episcopate (he died in 651), 'a hostile Mercian army under the leadership of Penda, which had
   been cruelly devastating the Northumbrian regions far and
   wide, reached the royal *urbs* called after a former Queen Bebba
   [Bamburgh]'.
9 Bede, *HE* iii.24. The *fluuium Uinued* was in West Yorkshire *in
   regione Loidis*, the region from which modern Leeds takes its
   name, but the location of the battle has not been identified; *HB*
   64 calls this battle *strages Gai campi*, 'slaughter of *campus Gai*'.
10 Yorke, *Kings and Kingdoms*, 78.
11 Bede, *HE* iii.14; iii.24.
12 *HB* 57 names Oswig's earlier wife as Rieinmelth daughter of
   Royth son of Rum.
13 Bede, *HE* iv.19 outlines the chronology of Ecgfrith and
   Aeðilthryð's marriage, but it is only in *ASC* where the
   foundation of Ely is dated to 673.

14 Bede, *HE* iii.14 hints at Alchfrith's fate, but otherwise he simply disappears from our sources without explanation. On the likelihood that Alchfrith's rebellion was spurred by the threat of Ecgfrith, see P. Wormald, 'The Age of Bede and Aethelbald', in J. Campbell (ed.), *The Anglo-Saxons* (London, 1991), 70–100, at 93.

15 Bede, *HE* iv.5. The accuracy of Bede's placement of Oswig's death in 670 has been a subject of doubt, but is supported by the king's obituary in AU 671.1 – see AU 680.4 (Battle of the Trent, 679), AU 685.2 (Berct's expedition, 684) and AU 686.1 (Dunnichen, 685) as showing that these events are consistently placed one year too late in the annals. K. Harrison, 'The Reign of King Ecgfrith of Northumbria', in *The Yorkshire Archaeological Journal* 43 (1971), 79–84, has pointed out that it is possible for Bede to have accurately preserved both the year of Oswig's death and Ecgfrith's regnal year at his death if we allow for the possibility that Ecgfrith's reign was not reckoned to have begun until sometime after 20 May 670.

16 Bede, *HE* iii.24.

17 Stephan, *VW*, 17. See also Yorke, *Kings and Kingdoms*, 83–84.

18 Stephan, *VW* 19 implies that this marriage had not yet broken up when the battle took place. The less satisfactory dating of this battle to 676 (see for example A.A.M. Duncan, *Scotland: The Making of the Kingdom* (Edinburgh, 1975), 53; P. Marren, *Grampian Battlefields: The Historic Battles of North East Scotland from AD 84 to 1745* (Aberdeen, 1990), 21) derives from the idea that an Irish annal notice in that year (AU 676.3) that 'many Picts were drowned in *Lann Abae*' might be a reference to the Two Rivers.

19 Stephan, *VW* 19; Bede, *HE* iii.24. On the relationship of this battle with Oswig's death, see A.P. Smyth, *Warlords and Holy Men: Scotland AD 80–1000* (Edinburgh, 1984), 62. The 'battle of Luith Feirn .i. in Fortriu' of AU 664.3 may well be a reference to an Oswegian campaign in which he 'overwhelmed and made tributary' the Picts (Bede, *HE* ii.5), but we cannot be certain about this.

20 AU 664.3; 693.1.

21 Drust f. Donuel appears in the 'Pictish' regnal list; on the
likelihood that this list was 'in origin… simply a *Fortriu*
regnal list', see Broun, 'Seven Kingdoms', 38. On the likelihood
that he was the Pictish captain at the Two Rivers, see
Anderson, *KKES*, 172.

22 Stephan, *VW* 19.

23 This subject has been broached by A. Woolf, 'Onuist son
of Uurguist: *tyrannus carnifex* or a David for the Picts?', in
M. Worthington and D. Hill (eds), *Æthelbald, Beornred and
Offa: the eighth-century kings of Mercia and their world* (Oxford,
forthcoming).

24 Stephan, *VW* 19.

25 AU 672.6. The annals appear to date events one year too late
at this point (cf. note 15 above).

26 FA §165. For other translations of the poem, see Skene, *Chron.
Picts & Scots*, 402; Anderson, *ESSH* 1, 194–95; T.O. Clancy (ed.)
The Triumph Tree: Scotland's Earliest Poetry, 550–1350 (Edinburgh,
1998), 115.

27 Anonymous, *Betha Adamnáin*, in M. Herbert and P. Ó Riain
(eds), *Betha Adamnáin: The Irish Life of Adamnán* (London, Irish
Texts Society, 1988), §14.

28 Anderson, *KKES*, 171; see also M. Miller, 'Eanfrith's Pictish
Son', in *Northern History* 14 (1978), 47–66, at 52. For the
genealogical tract, see Anderson, *ESSH* 1, p. clviii, with
correction noted in Anderson, *KKES*, 245 (n.70).

29 ACamb 627, although we cannot be certain that this Belin is
Beli map Neithon.

30 *HB* 57.

31 A. Woolf, 'Pictish matriliny reconsidered', in *Innes Review* 49
(1998), 147–67, at 161–62.

32 See for example F.M. Stenton, *Anglo-Saxon England* (Oxford,
1947, second edition), 87. On Eanfrith and Talorcan see Bede,
HE iii.1; AU 632.1; 657.3.

33 Anderson, *KKES*, 169 (followed by Cruickshank, *Dunnichen*,
10); D.P. Kirby, '…per universas Pictorum provincias', in G.
Bonner (ed.), *Famulus Christi: Essays in Commemoration of the
Thirteenth Centenary of the Birth of the Venerable Bede* (London,
1976), 286–324, at 308 (followed by Miller, 'Eanfrith's Pictish

Son', 56). The chronology of the former model in particular, which requires Bridei to have been two generations further removed from Aeðilfrith than Ecgfrith, strains credulity.

34 See in particular Smyth, *Warlords*, 57–75; Woolf, 'Matriliny', *passim*; A. Ross, 'Pictish Matriliny?', in *Northern Studies* 34 (1999), 11–22. The matrilineal model dies hard, but it is encouraging that it has been rejected by I. Armit, *Celtic Scotland* (London, 1997), 77 and S.M. Foster, *Picts, Gaels and Scots: Early Historic Scotland* (London, 1996), 37, the two relevant works in Historic Scotland's series of general histories.

35 Woolf, 'Matriliny', 162.

36 AI 685; *HB* 57.

37 Woolf, 'Matriliny', 162; *idem*, 'Verturian Hegemony', 108. For a very different view of Bridei's background, see Smyth, *Warlords*, 63–65.

38 Bede, *HE* ii.12. See also York, *Kings and Kingdoms*, 77.

39 *ASC* 675 records that Wulfhere fought the West Saxons in 675, and so it may be thought unlikely that he fought with Ecgfrith in that year.

40 Stephan, *VW* 20.

41 Stephan, *VW* 19–20.

42 On the month in which the battle was fought, see Harrison, 'Reign of King Ecgfrith', 81.

43 Bede, *HE* iv.21; Stephan, *VW* 24; AU 680.4.

44 Bede, *HE* iv.12; iv.21.

45 Bede, *VCP* 27; *HE* iv.26.

46 Marren, *Grampian Battlefields*, 21.

47 Yorke, *Kings and Kingdoms*, 79.

48 Stephan, *VW* 19.

49 Stephan, *VW* 24.

50 AU 681.5; 682.4; 683.3. Any or all of these dates might be placed a year too late like Dunnichen (AU 686.1).

51 Woolf, 'Onuist son of Uurguist'; *idem*, 'Verturian Hegemony', 108–09.

52 Bede, *VCP* 27.

53 Bede, *HE* iii.4. For more on this see J.E. Fraser, 'Ministry, Mission, and Myth in Early Christian Fortriu', unpublished PhD thesis (forthcoming), especially chapter 6.

54 Fraser, 'Early Christian Fortriu', chapter 6.

55 Smyth, *Warlords*, 65–66. See also Marren, *Grampian Battlefields*, 21; Yorke, *Kings and Kingdoms*, 84–85.

56 Woolf, 'Matriliny', 162.

57 Cruickshank, *Dunnichen*, 8.

58 Bede, *HE* iii.21.

59 Yorke, *Kings and Kingdoms*, 82.

Chapter Three

1 Anon., *VCA* iv.8.

2 Anon., *VCA* iv.8.

3 Bede, *VCP* 27.

4 *HR* §1. For an English translation of this work see J. Stevenson (ed.), *Simeon of Durham: A History of the Kings of England* (Lampeter, 1987). This commentator has demonstrably mistakenly conflated the injustices of the Dunnichen campaign with those of the Irish expedition of 684.

5 R.P. Abels, *Lordship and Military Obligation in Anglo-Saxon England* (London, 1988), 11.

6 Bede, *HE* iv.26.

7 Smyth, *Warlords*, 66. The context into which Smyth places Dunnichen here varies significantly from my own.

8 Marren, *Grampian Battlefields*, 23.

9 Cruickshank, *Dunnichen*, 13.

10 Cruickshank, *Dunnichen*, 13. See also Smyth, *Warlords*, 66.

11 Cruickshank, *Dunnichen*, 12. This view follows Stephan without considering the likelihood that the latter is exaggerating the nature of Ecgfrith's lordship over the Picts.

12 Cruickshank, 'Dunnichen and Aberlemno', 72; *idem*, *Dunnichen*, 13.

13 Marren, *Grampian Battlefields*, 21.

14 Bede, *HE* iv.26; Stenton, *Anglo-Saxon England*, 87.

15 Bede, *HE* iv.26. Stenton, *Anglo-Saxon England*, 87 proposed that Oswig had annexed 'much Pictish territory', but our

evidence, in the form of references to Anglian interests in Stirling, Abercorn and among the *Niduari* of Fife, suggests that direct Northumbrian control may not have extended further north than the Ochils.

16 Stephan, *VW* 24.

17 Bede, *HE* iv.26; AU 685.2. Berctred was the *dux regius Nordanhymbrorum* killed fighting the Picts in 698 (Bede, HE v.24).

18 T.M. Charles-Edwards, *Early Christian Ireland* (Cambridge, 2000), 433–34.

19 AClon 680.

20 Charles-Edwards, *Early Christian Ireland*, 433n, suggests that 'they probably came from the Isle of Man, subject to Northumbria since Edwin's reign, or Rheged, subject since at least *c.* 650'; H. Moisl, 'The Bernician Royal Dynasty and the Irish in the Seventh Century', in *Peritia* 2 (1983), 103–26, at 120–24, suggests rather doubtfully that 'Britaines' here might refer to any inhabitants of Britain, including Gaelic- or Pictish-speakers.

21 Yorke, *Kings and Kingdoms*, 85; Charles-Edwards, *Early Christian Ireland*, 433.

22 On these hostages see AU 687.5.

23 Stenton, *Anglo-Saxon England*, 87; Moisl, 'Bernician Royal Dynasty and the Irish', 120–24.

24 Anon., *VCA* iii.6, written when Aldfrith was still king, provides the earliest hint that his parentage was of some doubt, suggesting that his sister Aelfflæd needed to be reminded of his existence and his relationship to her. Bede, *VCP* 24, says in his version of this same episode only that Aldfrith 'was said to be a son of [Ecgfrith's] father' (*ferebatur filius fuisse patris illius*), leaving room for doubt even about whether he was really 'his bastard brother' (*frater eius nothus*).

25 FA §165.

26 Bede, *HE* iv.26.

27 FA §165.

28 Oram, *Angus*, 77.

29 Féichín died of the pandemic illness *buide Chonaill* in 665 (AU 665.3; AI 666.5); *Vita sancti Fechini abbatis de Fauoria*, in

C. Plummer (ed.), *Vitae Sanctorum Hiberniae*, Vol. II, (Dublin, 1997), 76–86, makes him Abbot of Fore. For the identification of Vigean with Féichín, see W.J. Watson, *The History of the Celtic Place-Names of Scotland* (Edinburgh, 1926), 321–22.

30 Cruickshank, *Dunnichen*, 9.

31 Wormald, 'Age of Bede and Aethelbald', 94; Yorke, *Kings and Kingdoms*, 85.

Chapter Four

1 Bede, *HE* iv.27–28. Cuthbert, of course, later switched sees with Eata and returned to Lindisfarne, but his visit to Carlisle at the time of Ecgfrith's death indicates that he was still Bishop of Hexham in May 685.

2 Bede, *HE* iv.28.

3 The inscription 'on the ninth day of the Kalends of May in the fifteenth year of the reign of King Ecfrid' is recorded in R. Cramp, *Corpus of Anglo-Saxon Stone Sculpture in England*, Vol. I: *County Durham and Northumberland* (Oxford, 1984), 113.

4 Stephan, *VW* 19–20; that Stephan's use of *parilis* in the latter chapter refers back to the *equitatus exercitus* of the former has been established by N.J. Higham, 'Cavalry in Early Bernicia?', in *Northern History* 27 (1991), 236–41, at 238.

5 Adomnán, *VC* i.8.

6 Abels, *Lordship and Military Obligation*, 36.

7 Abels, *Lordship and Military Obligation*, 32; for the terminology see Bede, *VCP* 27 (*tutores*); J. Campbell, 'Elements in the Background to the Life of St Cuthbert and his Early Cult', in G. Bonner, D. Rollason and C. Stancliffe (eds), *St Cuthbert, his Cult and his Community to AD 1200* (Woodbridge, 1989), 3–19, at 8 (*ministri*).

8 Abels, *Lordship and Military Obligation*, 32.

9 A concept deconstructed by Abels, *Lordship and Military Obligation*, 13–22.

10 Anon., *VCA* iii.6.

11 For examples of this principle put into practice, see Abels, *Lordship and Military Obligation*, 33.

12 Campbell, 'Background to the Life of St Cuthbert', 8. On Berctred's death in battle with the Picts, see Bede, *HE* v.24; on his relationship with Beornheth, see AU 698.2. It is possible that the kingdom over which Beornheth ruled as sub-king was formerly British territory in Lothian.

13 Wainwright, 'Nechtanesmere', 95; Cruickshank, *Dunnichen*, 17; Alcock, 'Dunnichen', 139.

14 Stephan, *VW* 34–38.

15 AU 638.1.

16 *HB* 64–65.

17 Smyth, *Warlords*, 67; Marren, *Grampian Battlefields*, 22. The death of *Domnall m. Auin, rex Alo Cluathe*, is recorded at AU 694.6. Unless intermediate reigns have not been recorded in the annals, Dumngual appears to have succeeded *Guret rex Alo Cluathe* in 658 (658.2) and to have reigned for about thirty-six years, during which time Dumbarton appears to have won decisive victories over Cenél Loairn of Dál Riata (AU 678.3) and the Cruithin of Co. Down (AU 682.2).

18 AU 678.3; 682.2. In both cases 'Britons' only are mentioned, though it is likely that the men of Dumbarton are referred to here.

19 Fraser, 'Early Christian Fortriu', chapter 4.

20 Marren, *Grampian Battlefields*, 24.

21 Campbell, 'Background to the Life of St Cuthbert', 4–5.

22 Marren, *Grampian Battlefields*, 23. There are no real grounds for accepting the identification of the Two Rivers as the Avon and the Carron in West Lothian (cf. Cruickshank, *Dunnichen*, 12; Marren, *Grampian Battlefields*, 24), which do not seem at the time to have been in Fortriu. My own hunch is that the Tay was one of the two rivers involved, but one can only speculate.

23 Wainwright, 'Nechtanesmere', 96; Cruickshank, *Dunnichen*, 17; Marren, *Grampian Battlefields*, 24; Alcock, 'Dunnichen', 141; Hooper, 'Aberlemno Stone', 192, envisions the alternative route 'up the east coast' without comment.

24 *The New Statistical Account of Scotland* (Edinburgh, 1845), vol. xi, 691.

Notes

25 J. Sinclair (ed.), *The Statistical Account of Scotland* (Edinburgh, 1791–99), vol. vi, 597, notes the fact that 'the loch of Forfar, upwards of twenty years ago, was drained of about sixteen feet perpendicular depth of water'. My understanding of the early historic landscape of Angus has been greatly improved as a result of conversation with Dr Richard Oram, for whose kind assistance I am grateful. Any errors in this understanding are, of course, my own responsibility.

26 Bede, *HE* iv.26.

27 Bede, *HE* iv.26.

28 Cruickshank, 'Dunnichen and Aberlemno', 72 and Marren, *Grampian Battlefields*, 23–24 follow Wainwright, 'Nechtanesmere', 86, 96 in imagining that the Northumbrians were 'in hot pursuit' of Picts in 'feigned flight' when battle was joined.

29 Tacitus, *Agricola* 26.

30 Stenton, *Anglo-Saxon England*, 88. See also Anderson, *KKES*, 173; Duncan, *Scotland*, 53.

31 Cruickshank, *Dunnichen*, 18; see also Wainwright, 'Nechtanesmere', 96; Marren, *Grampian Battlefields*, 24.

32 Tacitus, *Agricola* 29; Stephan, *VW* 19.

33 Oram, *Angus*, 79. The nature of the toponymic and (meagre) physical evidence relating to the presence of a *dún* on Dunnichen Hill are discussed by Wainwright, 'Nechtanesmere', 94–95 and Cruickshank, *Dunnichen*, 31.

34 Oram, *Angus*, 60. Kemp's Castle appears to have its origins in the Iron Age, and to have been in continuous use into the Pictish period. The name 'Camp Castle' is recorded in *New Stat. Acct.*, vol. xi, 632.

35 For a listing of these name-forms see Wainwright, 'Nechtanesmere', 86 (n26).

36 *Stat. Acct. Scot.*, vol. i, 420.

37 Wainwright, 'Nechtanesmere', 96; followed closely by Cruickshank, *Dunnichen*, 18–19.

38 For contemporary usage of these terms see AU 678.3 (*interfectio generis Loairnn*, 'slaughter of Cenél Loairn') and AU 704.1 (*strages Dal Riaiti*, 'slaughter of the Dál Riata').

39 Wainwright, 'Nechtanesmere', 96; again followed closely by Cruickshank, *Dunnichen*, 18–19.

40 Bede, *HE* iv.22.

41 A further potential problem with the traditional location of the battlefield involves evidence to suggest that it was a burial ground that was already ancient in 685. See *New Stat. Acct.*, vol. xi, 146–47 and the analysis of Wainwright, 'Nechtanesmere', 92–93.

42 For objections based on 'the place-name connection', see Cruickshank, 'Dunnichen and Aberlemno', 72 (n6) and, much earlier, Wainwright, 'Nechtanesmere', 88, who rejected the possibility that the battle was fought 'outside Dunnichen' or 'on the opposite side' of the hill (as locals then believed) on the grounds that it bore 'the name *Dún Nechtain* and the associated name *Nechtanesmere*'. Though Cruickshank finds this 'more compelling' than the 'persuasive' arguments put forward by Prof. Alcock, I do not find the place-name evidence conclusive and am led to the opposite conclusion.

43 Alcock, 'Dunnichen', 140–42. The quotation is from Marren, *Grampian Battlefields*, 1.

44. *Stat. Acct. Scot.*, vol. vi, 529. On George Dempster's efforts to drain Restenneth Loch and Dunnichen Moss, see Wainwright, 'Nechtanesmere', 90–91.

45 As demonstrated to me by R.D. Oram on a visit to the area.

46 *New Stat. Acct.*, vol. xi, 694.

47 *New Stat. Acct.*, vol. xi, 149; see also *Stat. Acct. Scot.*, vol. vi, 529.

48 *Stat. Acct. Scot.*, vol. vi, 529; there is no trace now of such stones, neither are they mentioned in *New Stat. Acct.*, though various finds of 'coins, urns, and pieces of armour' in this same area are mentioned, vol. xi, 694. At first glance these do not appear to speak of the Picts; nevertheless from the time of Buchanan this purported battle beside Loch Fithie was associated with them – albeit with a fanciful battle at the end of the Pictish period. It may be pointed out that *New Stat. Acct.*, vol. xi, 146, records that 'a confused tradition prevails of a great battle having been fought on the East Mains of Dunnichen', but as there is no trace of this in the older *Stat. Acct. Scot.*, one is inclined to wonder whether it was in fact the publication of Chalmers's identification of Dún Nechtain with Dunnichen that gave rise to this 'confused tradition'.

Chapter Five

1 The most comprehensive recent reconstruction of this kind has been that of Marren, *Grampian Battlefields*, 24–26.

2 Cruickshank, 'Dunnichen and Aberlemno', 72 (n6) has put forward the first rejection in print of Professor Alcock's arguments since they were published in 1996. As noted above, I am not convinced by 'the place-name connection' which forms the grounds of Mr Cruickshank's objections here.

3 On locating *Mons Graupius* see Marren, *Grampian Battlefields*, 12–18.

4 On locating Maldon see J.M. Dodgson, 'The Site of the Battle of Maldon', in D. Scragg (ed.), *The Battle of Maldon AD 991* (Oxford, 1991), 170–79.

5 Alcock, 'Dunnichen', 140–42.

6 The engagement is described as a *bellum* rather than an *obsessio*; for scepticism about the role of any hill-fort in the battle, see Alcock, 'Dunnichen', 136–38.

7 The 'visible remains of the foundation of some ancient building' on the south side of Dunnichen Hill were noted in *Stat. Acct. Scot.*, vol. vi, 419; these same remains are described as 'a fort built with dry stone, without any cement' in *New Stat. Acct.*, vol. xi, 142, where it is recorded (p. 146) that 'the stones... have been removed to build fences; and its area has been nearly obliterated by a quarry'.

8 Stephan, *VW* 19.

9 The identification of particular figures in the Aberlemno battle-scene as Pictish and Anglian has been established most thoroughly by Cruickshank, 'Dunnichen and Aberlemno', 78–80; see also Hooper, 'Aberlemno Stone', 191. It would seem necessary, given Marren's casual reference (*Grampian Battlefields*, 24) to 'the mass of painted warriors', to point out that the battle-scene makes no suggestion whatever that the Picts memorialised in it had painted themselves.

10 D. Scragg (ed.), *The Battle of Maldon*, ll. 17–21, in Scragg (ed.), *Battle of Maldon*, 18–30.

11 Stephan, *VW* 19.

12 Cruickshank, 'Dunnichen and Aberlemno', 84. We need not assume that each Anglian figure in the battle-scene depicts Ecgfrith, although that is certainly as valid an interpretation as any; see Cessford, 'Cavalry in Early Bernicia', 185; Hooper, 'Aberlemno Stone', 192.

13 Cruickshank, *Dunnichen*, 19.

14 Cruickshank, *Dunnichen*, 6, 19.

15 *The Battle of Maldon*, ll. 30–61.

16 Marren, *Grampian Battlefields*, 23.

17 Bede, *HE* iii.14.

18 Campbell, 'Background to the Life of St Cuthbert', 10.

19 Anon., *VCA* iv.8. It is commonly said that the battle took place at three o'clock.

20 Marren, *Grampian Battlefields*, 2.

21 Higham, 'Cavalry in Early Bernicia?', 236–41 raised doubts about this without considering the evidence of the Aberlemno battle-scene, to which both Cessford, 'Cavalry in Early Bernicia', 185, and Hooper, 'Aberlemno Stone', 190–91 make reference in raising creditable objections to Higham's position.

22 Tacitus, *Agricola* 35.

23 Anderson, *KKES*, 173.

24 Alcock, 'Dunnichen', 141.

25 Tacitus, *Agricola* 36.

26 Cruickshank, 'Dunnichen and Aberlemno', 82.

27 *The Battle of Maldon*, ll. 106–10.

28 Cessford, 'Cavalry in Early Bernicia', 185–86 interprets the Anglian figures in the battle-scene as throwing javelins, while Hooper, 'Aberlemno Stone', 191 allows for 'either a depiction of a thrusting or a throwing action'.

29 *Gweith Gwen Ystrat*, l. 10, in J.T. Koch, *The Gododdin of Aneirin: Text and Context from Dark-Age North Britain* (Cardiff & Andover, 1997), pp.xxvii–viii.

30 Tacitus, *Agricola* 36.

31 Cruickshank, 'Dunnichen and Aberlemno', 84, suggests that there were real differences in the sizes of Pictish and Northumbrian horses, but it may be that the sculptor had artistic reasons for showing such differences.

32 Cruickshank, 'Dunnichen and Aberlemno', 80–81.

33 Tacitus, *Agricola* 36.

34 *Gweith Gwen Ystrat*, ll. 7, 12.

35 Tacitus, *Agricola* 37.

36 Tacitus, *Agricola* 37.

37 *Gweith Gwen Ystrat*, ll. 12–16.

38 Cruickshank, 'Dunnichen and Aberlemno', 82. Such an interpretation requires us to suppose that our Pictish sculptor was not attempting to provide his audience with a snapshot of a single moment in time in this part of the scene, but was instead trying to show more than one aspect of the battle in a single set of figures.

39 Stephan, *VW* 19.

40 Cruickshank, 'Dunnichen and Aberlemno', 80–81.

41 Tacitus, *Agricola* 37.

42 Bede, *HE* iv.26.

43 *Gweith Gwen Ystrat*, ll. 17–21. There is room for doubt in some of these translations.

44 *Gweith Gwen Ystrat*, l. 22.

45 Bede, *VCP* 27.

46 FA §165.

47 Alcock, 'Dunnichen', 133.

48 Cruickshank, *Dunnichen*, 25, envisions *Iniu feras Bruide cath* to be part of one such song.

49 *The Battle of Maldon*, ll. 127–97. See also R. Abels, 'English Tactics, Strategy and Military Organization in the Late Tenth Century', in Scragg (ed.), *Battle of Maldon*, 143–55, at 151–52.

50 Cruickshank, 'Dunnichen and Aberlemno', 84–85.

51 *The Battle of Maldon*, ll. 185–97; 202–325.

52 Bede, *HE* iv.26.

53 Bede, *HE* iv.26.

54 Stephan, *VW* 19.

55 Tacitus, *Agricola* 37.

56 *Gweith Gwen Ystrat* ll. 23–26, 8–9.

57 Bede, *HE* iv.26.

58 Cruickshank, *Dunnichen*, 19.

59 Marren, *Grampian Battlefields*, 2.

60 Wainwright, 'Nechtanesmere', 86 interprets this same passage

as suggesting that most of the survivors 'no doubt saved
themselves by flight'.

Chapter Six

1   Adomnán, *VC* ii.46.

2   Bede, *VCP* 27.

3   Anon., *VCA* iv.8.

4   Stephan, *VW* 44.

5   See Yorke, *Kings and Kingdoms*, 80.

6   Bede, *VCP* 24.

7   Bede, *HE* iv.22.

8   N. Macdougall, *James IV* (East Linton, 1997), 275–76.

9   Bede, *HE* iv.22.

10 Bede, *HE* iv.22.

11 *HED* 9.

12 Fraser, 'Early Christian Fortriu', chapter 6. The late source in
    question is Anonymous, *Betha Adamnáin*, §14.

13 R.I. Best and H.J. Lawlor (eds), *The Martyrology of Tallaght*
    (Henry Bradshaw Society 68: London, 1931), 27 May
    (*Echbritan mac Óssu*). The king's name was also inserted
    into the contemporary (*c.* 800) martyrology of Óengus at
    some later date, though on 25 May; W. Stokes (ed.) *Félire
    Óengusso Céli Dé – The Martyrology of Oengus the Culdee*
    (Henry Bradshaw Society 29: London, 1905). The twelfth-
    century Gorman martyrology, however, follows the Tallaght
    commemoration on 27 May, W. Stokes (ed.) *Félire Húi
    Gormáin – The Martyrology of Gorman* (Henry Bradshaw
    Society 9: London, 1895). Reeves, in J.H. Todd and W. Reeves
    (eds), *The Martyrology of Donegal: A Calendar of the Saints of
    Ireland* (Dublin, 1864), 140–41, protested that 'it is difficult,
    however, to understand how he came to be regarded as a
    saint', suggesting that the text 'is probably in error' in making
    him *mac Ossu* because 27 May was not the day of Ecgfrith's
    death ('independently of his unsaintly character and hostility
    to the Irish, the discrepancy of the dates seems to exclude

him [Ecgfrith] from the present commemoration'). Exactly
how, where, and on what basis Ecgfrith was culted as a saint
remains quite obscure – more remarkable still is the striking
rapprochement between his cult and Ireland that caused
Reeves such shock.

14 Bede, *HE* iv.26.
15 Stephan, *VW* 24.
16 Bede, *HE* iv.26.
17 Bede, *HE* iv.26.
18 Wainwright, 'Nechtanesmere', 97.
19 Cruickshank, *Dunnichen*, 23. See also Cruickshank's discussion
   of nineteenth- and twentieth-century historiography at 37–39.
20 David Henry, foreword to Cruickshank, *Dunnichen* (1991
   edition), 3.
21 Cruickshank, *Dunnichen*, 36.
22 Marren, *Grampian Battlefields*, 22.
23 Yorke, *Kings and Kingdoms*, 91.
24 Marren, *Grampian Battlefields*, 21.
25 Marren, *Grampian Battlefields*, 26.
26 Anon., *VCA* iii.6.
27 Smyth, *Warlords*, 65–66.
28 Wainwright, 'Nechtanesmere', 97, where the crucial role
   played by the Mercians in the fate of Northumbria is
   recognised.
29 Campbell, 'Background to the Life of St Cuthbert', 6–7.
30 *HB* 57.
31 Bede, *HE* v.24; AU 698.2; 711.3.
32 Marren, *Grampian Battlefields*, 26.
33 Bede, *HE* v.23.
34 Yorke, *Kings and Kingdoms*, 169.
35 On the likelihood that Northumbrian political instability was
   a key factor in curtailing imperial ambitions, see Duncan,
   Scotland, 62.
36 Cruickshank, *Dunnichen*, 21.
37 Wainwright, 'Nechtanesmere', 97.
38 Marren, *Grampian Battlefields*, 20.
39 Fraser, 'Early Christian Fortriu', chapter 7.
40 G.W.S. Barrow, 'The Childhood of Scottish Christianity: a

Note on Some Place-Name Evidence', in *Scottish Studies* 27 (1983), 1–15, at 8; for the building of the church, see Bede, *HE* v.21. The basis for such an identification is a property called *Egglespether* ('church of Peter'), which went with the church that was rebuilt as Restenneth Priory church in the middle of the twelfth century.

41 On the relationship between Aberlemno and Restenneth (in 1624) see *New Stat. Acct.*, vol. xi, 695.

Chapter Seven

1 Marren, *Grampian Battlefields*, 2; Cruickshank, *Dunnichen*, 42.
2 Cruickshank, *Dunnichen*, 44.
3 *Stat. Acct. Scot.*, vol. vi, 521; *New Stat. Acct.*, vol. xi, 692, 632.
4 Wainwright, 'Nechtanesmere', 94.
5 *New Stat. Acct.*, vol. xi, 146; see also *Stat. Acct. Scot.*, vol. i, 419.
6 Wainwright, 'Nechtanesmere', 94.
7 Cruickshank, *Dunnichen*, 6; Wainwright, 'Nechtanesmere', 85.

Bibliography

Abels, Richard P. *Lordship and Military Obligation in Anglo-Saxon England*. London, 1988.

Abels, Richard. 'English Tactics, Strategy and Military Organization in the Late Tenth Century', in Scragg (ed.), *Battle of Maldon*, 143–55.

Adomnán. *Vita Columbae*, in Alan Orr Anderson and Marjorie Ogilvie Anderson (eds), *Adomnán's Life of Columba*. Oxford, 1991.

Alcock, Leslie. 'The Site of the "Battle of Dunnichen"', in *The Scottish Historical Review* 75 (1996), 130–42.

Anderson, Marjorie O. *Kings and Kingship in Early Scotland*. Edinburgh and London, 1973.

Anonymous, *Betha Adamnáin*, in Máire Herbert and Pádraig Ó Riain (eds), *Betha Adamnáin: The Irish Life of Adamnán*. London, Irish Texts Society, 1988.

Anonymous. *Vita Sancti Cudberti*, in B. Colgrave (ed.), *Two Lives of Saint Cuthbert*. Cambridge, 1940.

Armit, Ian. *Celtic Scotland*. London, 1997.

Barrow, G.W.S. 'The Childhood of Scottish Christianity: a Note on Some Place-Name Evidence', in *Scottish Studies* 27 (1983), 1–15.

Bede, *Historia Ecclesiastica Gentis Anglorum*, in B. Colgrave and R.A.B. Mynors (eds), *Bede's Ecclesiastical History of the English People*. Oxford, 1991.

Bede, *Vita Sancti Cuthberti*, in B. Colgrave (ed.), *Two Lives of Saint Cuthbert*. Cambridge, 1940.

Best, Richard Irvine and Hugh Jackson Lawlor (eds), *The Martyrology of Tallaght*. Henry Bradshaw Society 68: London, 1931.

Broun, Dauvit. 'The Seven Kingdoms in De situ Albanie: A Record of Pictish political Geography of imaginary Map of ancient Alba?', in Cowan and McDonald (eds), *Alba*, 24–42.

Campbell, J. 'Elements in the Background to the Life of St Cuthbert and his Early Cult', in G. Bonner, D. Rollason and C. Stancliffe (eds), *St Cuthbert, his Cult and his Community to AD 1200*. Woodbridge, 1989, 3–19.

Campbell, James (ed.), *The Anglo-Saxons*. London, 1991.

Charles-Edwards, T.M. *Early Christian Ireland*. Cambridge, 2000.

Cessford, C. 'Cavalry in Early Bernicia: a reply', in *Northern History* 79 (1993), 185–87.

Cowan, Edward J. and R. Andrew McDonald (eds), *Alba: Celtic Scotland in the Middle Ages*. East Linton, 2000.

Cramp, Rosemary. *Corpus of Anglo-Saxon Stone Sculpture in England*, vol. I: *County Durham and Northumberland*. Oxford, 1984.

Cruickshank, Graeme. *The Battle of Dunnichen*. Balgavies, 1999.

Cruickshank, Graeme D.R. 'The Battle of Dunnichen and the Aberlemno Battle-Scene', in Cowan and McDonald (eds), *Alba*, 69–87.

Dodgson, John McN. 'The Site of the Battle of Maldon', in Scragg (ed.), *Battle of Maldon*, 170–79.

Duncan, A.A.M. *Scotland: The Making of the Kingdom*. Edinburgh, 1975.

Forsyth, Katherine. *Language in Pictland: the case against 'non-Indo-European Pictish'*. Utrecht, 1997.

Foster, Sally M. *Picts, Gaels and Scots: Early Historic Scotland*. London, 1996.

Fraser, James E. 'Ministry, Mission, and Myth in Early Christian Fortriu'. Unpublished PhD thesis. University of Edinburgh (forthcoming).

Harrison, Kenneth. 'The Reign of King Ecgfrith of Northumbria', in *The Yorkshire Archaeological Journal* 43 (1971), 79–84.

Bibliography

Higham, N.J. 'Cavalry in Early Bernicia?', in *Northern History* 27 (1991), 236–41.

Historia Dunelmensis Ecclesiae, attributed to Simeon of Durham, Thomas Arnold (ed.), *Symeonis Monachi Opera Omnia*, vol. I. Edinburgh, 1882.

Historia Regum, attributed to Simeon of Durham, in Thomas Arnold (ed.), *Symeonis Monachi Opera Omnia*, vol. II. Edinburgh, 1882.

Hooper, Nicholas. 'The Aberlemno Stone and Cavalry in Anglo-Saxon England', in *Northern History* 79 (1993), 188–96.

Jackson, K.H. 'The Pictish Language', in F.T. Wainwright (ed.), *The Problem of the Picts*. Edinburgh, 1955, 129–66.

Kirby, D.P. '…per universas Pictorum provincias', in Gerald Bonner (ed.), *Famulus Christi: Essays in Commemoration of the Thirteenth Centenary of the Birth of the Venerable Bede*. London, 1976, 286–324.

Koch, John Thomas. *The* Gododdin *of Aneirin: Text and Context from Dark-Age North Britain*. Cardiff and Andover, 1997.

Mac Airt, Seán and Gearóid mac Niocaill (eds), *The Annals of Ulster (to A.D. 1131)*. Dublin, 1983.

Macdougall, Norman. *James IV*. East Linton, 1997.

Marren, Peter. *Grampian Battlefields: The Historic Battles of North East Scotland from AD84 to 1745*. Aberdeen, 1990.

Miller, Molly. 'Eanfrith's Pictish Son', in *Northern History* 14 (1978), 47–66.

Moisl, Hermann. 'The Bernician Royal Dynasty and the Irish in the Seventh Century', in *Peritia* 2 (1983), 103–26.

Morris, John (ed.), *Nennius: British History and the Welsh Annals*. London and Chichester, 1980.

Murphy, Denis (ed.), *The Annals of Clonmacnoise*. Llanerch, 1993.

The New Statistical Account of Scotland (Edinburgh, 1845).

Oram, Richard. *Angus & the Mearns: a Historical Guide*. Edinburgh, 1996.

Plummer, Charles (ed.), *Vitae Sanctorum Hiberniae*, vol. II. Dublin, 1997.

Radner, Joan Newlon (ed.), *Fragmentary Annals of Ireland*. Dublin, 1978.

Ritchie, Anna. *Picts: an Introduction to the Life of the Picts and the Carved Stones in the Care of Historic Scotland*. Edinburgh, 1989.

Romilly Allen, J. and Joseph Anderson, *The Early Christian Monuments of Scotland*. Balgavies, 1993.

Ross, Alasdair. 'Pictish Matriliny?', in *Northern Studies* 34 (1999), 11–22.

Scragg, Donald (ed.), *The Battle of Maldon*, in Scragg (ed.), *Battle of Maldon*, 15–36.

Scragg, Donald (ed.), *The Battle of Maldon AD 991*. Oxford, 1991.

Sinclair, John (ed.), *The Statistical Account of Scotland* (Edinburgh, 1791–99).

Smyth, Alfred P. *Warlords and Holy Men: Scotland AD 80–1000*. Edinburgh, 1984.

Stenton, F.M. *Anglo-Saxon England*. Oxford, 1947 (second edition).

Stephan, *Vita Sancti Wilfrithi*, in B. Colgrave (ed.), *The Life of Bishop Wilfrid by Eddius Stephanus*. Cambridge, 1927.

Stokes, Whitley (ed.), *The Annals of Tigernach*, vol. 1. Lampeter, 1993.

Stokes, Whitley (ed.) *Félire Húi Gormáin – The Martyrology of Gorman*. Henry Bradshaw Society 9: London, 1895.

Stokes, Whitley (ed.) *Félire Óengusso Céli Dé – The Martyrology of Oengus the Culdee*. Henry Bradshaw Society 29: London, 1905.

Swanton, Michael (ed.), *The Anglo-Saxon Chronicles*. London, 2000.

Tacitus, *De Vita Agricolae*, in R.M. Ogilvie and Sir Ian Richmond (eds), *Cornelii Taciti De Vita Agricolae*. Oxford, 1967.

Todd, James Henthorn and William Reeves (eds), *The Martyrology of Donegal: A Calendar of the Saints of Ireland*. Dublin, 1864.

Wainwright, F.T. 'Nechtanesmere', in *Antiquity* 86 (1948), 82–97.

Watson, William J. *The History of the Celtic Place-Names of Scotland*. Edinburgh, 1926.

Woolf, Alex. 'Pictish matriliny reconsidered', in *Innes Review* 49 (1998), 147–67.

Woolf, Alex. 'The Verturian Hegemony: A Mirror in the North', in M.P. Brown and C.A. Farr (eds), *Mercia: An Anglo-Saxon Kingdom in Europe*. Leicester and New York, 2001, 106–11.

Wormald, Patrick. 'The Age of Bede and Aethelbald', in J.
Campbell (ed.), *The Anglo-Saxons*. London, 1991, 70–100.
Yorke, Barbara. *Kings and Kingdoms of Early Anglo-Saxon England*.
London and New York, 1990.

List of Illustrations

All photographs from the author's collection unless otherwise stated.

Index

TEMPUS – REVEALING HISTORY

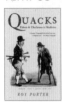
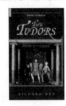

Quacks Fakers and Charlatans in Medicine
ROY PORTER

'A delightful book' *The Daily Telegraph*
'Hugely entertaining' *BBC History Magazine*

£12.99   0 7524 2590 0

The Tudors
RICHARD REX

'Up-to-date, readable and reliable. The best
introduction to England's most important dynasty'
David Starkey
'Vivid, entertaining... quite simply the best short
introduction' *Eamon Duffy*
'Told with enviable narrative skill... a delight for
any reader' *THES*

£9.99   0 7524 3333 4

The Kings & Queens of England
MARK ORMROD

'Of the numerous books on the kings and queens
of England, this is the best'
Alison Weir

£9.99   0 7524 2598 6

The Covent Garden Ladies
Pimp General Jack & the Extraordinary Story of Harris's List
HALLIE RUBENHOLD

'Sex toys, porn... forget Ann Summers, Miss Love
was at it 250 years ago' *The Times*
'Compelling' *The Independent on Sunday*
'Marvellous' *Leonie Frieda*
'Filthy' *The Guardian*

£9.99   0 7524 3739 9

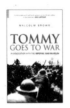
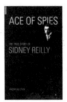

Okinawa 1945
GEORGE FEIFER

'A great book... Feifer's account of the three sides
and their experiences far surpasses most books
about war'
Stephen Ambrose

£17.99   0 7524 3324 5

Tommy Goes To War
MALCOLM BROWN

'A remarkably vivid and frank account of the
British soldier in the trenches'
Max Arthur
'The fury, fear, mud, blood, boredom and bravery
that made up life on the Western Front are vividly
presented and illustrated'
The Sunday Telegraph

£12.99   0 7524 2980 4

Ace of Spies The True Story of Sidney Reilly
ANDREW COOK

'The most definitive biography of the spying ace
yet written... both a compelling narrative and a
myth-shattering *tour de force*'
Simon Sebag Montefiore
'The absolute last word on the subject' *Nigel West*
'Makes poor 007 look like a bit of a wuss'
The Mail on Sunday

£12.99   0 7524 2959 0

Sex Crimes
From Renaissance to Enlightenment
W.M. NAPHY

'Wonderfully scandalous'
Diarmaid MacCulloch

£10.99   0 7524 2977 9

TEMPUS REVEALING HISTORY

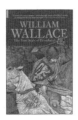 

William Wallace
The True Story of Braveheart
CHRIS BROWN
'The truth about Braveheart' *The Scottish Daily Mail*
£17.99
0 7524 3432 2

The Roman Conquest of Scotland
The Battle of Mons Graupius AD 84
JAMES E. FRASER
'Challenges a long held view' *The Scottish Sunday Express*
£17.99
0 7524 3325 3

An Abundance of Witches
The Great Scottish Witch-Hunt
P.G. MAXWELL-STUART
'An amazing account of Scots women in league with the Devil' *The Sunday Post*
£17.99
0 7524 3329 6

Scottish Voices from the Great War
DEREK YOUNG
'A treasure trove of personal letters and diaries from the archives'
   Trevor Royle
£17.99
0 7524 3326 1

 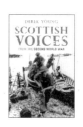

Culloden
The Last Charge of the Highland Clans
JOHN SADLER
£25
0 7524 3955 3

The Pictish Conquest
The Battle of Dunnichen 685 & the Birth of Scotland
JAMES E. FRASER
£12.99

The Scottish Civil War
The Bruces & the Balliols & the War for the Control of Scotland
MICHAEL PENMAN
'A highly informative and engaging account' *Historic Scotland*
£16.99
0 7524 2319 3

Scottish Voices from the Second World War
DEREK YOUNG
'Poignant memories of a lost generation… heart-rending' *The Sunday Post*
£17.99
0 7524 3710 0

TEMPUS REVEALING HISTORY

Scotland
From Prehistory to the Present
FIONA WATSON
The Scotsman **Bestseller**
£9.99
0 7524 2591 9

1314 Bannockburn
ARYEH NUSBACHER
'Written with good-humoured verve as
befits a rattling "yarn of sex, violence and
terror"'
History Scotland
£9.99
0 7524 2982 5

Flodden
NIALL BARR
'Tells the story brilliantly'
The Sunday Post
£9.99
0 7524 2593 5

Scotland's Black Death
The Foul Death of the English
KAREN JILLINGS
'So incongruously enjoyable a read, and so
attractively presented by the publishers'
The Scotsman
£14.99
0 7524 2314 2

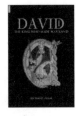

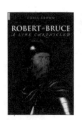

David I The King Who Made Scotland
RICHARD ORAM
'Enthralling... sets just the right tone as the
launch-volume of an important new series
of royal biographies' *Magnus Magnusson*
£17.99
0 7524 2825 X

The Kings & Queens of Scotland
RICHARD ORAM
'A serious, readable work that sweeps across
a vast historical landscape' *The Daily Mail*
£12.99
0 7524 3814 X

The Second Scottish Wars of Independence 1332–1363
CHRIS BROWN
'Explodes the myth of the invincible Bruces...
lucid and highly readable' *History Scotland*
£12.99
0 7524 3812 3

Robert the Bruce: A Life Chronicled
CHRIS BROWN
'A masterpiece of research'
The Scots Magazine
£30
0 7524 2575 7